LOVE, SEX, & FEMINISM

JOHN WILSON

LOVE, SEX, & FEMINISM

A PHILOSOPHICAL ESSAY

PRAEGER

PRAEGER SPECIAL STUDIES • PRAEGER SCIENTIFIC

Library of Congress Cataloging in Publication Data

Wilson, John, 1928-
   Love, sex, and feminism.

   Bibliography: p.
   Includes index.
   1. Sex. 2. Sex--Psychology. 3. Feminism.
4. Femininity (Psychology) I. Title.
HQ12.W54   301.41   79-24902
ISBN 0-03-056103-5

√ HQ
12
. W 54

Published in 1980 by Praeger Publishers
CBS Educational and Professional Publishing
A Division of CBS, Inc.
521 Fifth Avenue, New York, New York 10017 U.S.A.

© 1980 by Praeger Publishers

0123456789   038   987654321

Printed in the United States of America

PREFACE

There are several reasons why it is important to get clear about sexuality and its attendant concepts—apart, that is, from the general desirability of getting clear about anything that seems obscure and might be important. First, and perhaps most obviously, almost everybody is, in theory, involved in sexuality (even if only the sexuality of other people. Judging from certain symptoms, not everything is well in this area. Second, a great mass of practical, advisory, and pornographic literature (not to mention other media) deluges people, and it is clear that much of what is written and otherwise represented—I think, almost everything above the level of the strictly physiological—is dominated by certain conceptual or philosophical pictures, usually unconscious and nearly always incorrect. Third, there are reasons (philosophical reasons) for believing that sexuality is not a kind of optional exercise but something both inevitable and inevitably important for human beings. So, it is impossible to hold that the whole thing is a fuss about nothing, or about nothing necessarily important. Unlike gold, advertising, nationalism, and other hobbies, sex has a central and permanent place in human life.

Philosophers have, on the whole, given sex a bad deal—perhaps regarding it as unworthy of philosophical attention or, more probably, because the conceptual work required is extremely difficult. Even Plato's *Symposium*, despite its charms, seems plainly to lead in the wrong direction; and most subsequent writers of interest have not been philosophers (Stendhal, Freud, and so on). I aim here, therefore, simply to lay some of the foundations in this area. An enormous amount remains to be said even at the strictly philosophical level.

I said above "sexuality and its attendant concepts," but of course one very difficult problem is to decide just what concepts do in fact attend on sexuality. There is, however, some possibility of distinguishing, albeit very roughly, between two sorts of questions. Some involve sexuality or eroticism itself— these I try to answer in Part I. Others, which may be attached to a different sense of 'sex' (as when we talk of the male or female sex), are tied up with areas nowadays bearing titles such as "feminism" or "sexism"—they spill over into political questions of a more general kind but retain a common thread. These appear in Part II.

Some readers (perhaps particularly in North America) may, to judge from the literature, regard many of the issues that might come under the general title of 'feminism' as already settled. I can only persuade them that this is not so by what I have to say in Part II. Readers in European and other less "liberated" countries, on the other hand, might regard feminism as a passing fashion, not worthy of serious philosophical attention, or, more sophisticatedly, maintain it gives rise to no *specific* philosophical problems (that the problems had better be tackled under the usual philosophical headings—ethics, philosophy of mind, and so forth). Either of these views would be badly mistaken. This, too, I hope to show in the main text; but it is perhaps worth saying in advance that the concepts involved in being a woman or a man, like other concepts attendant on sexuality, play a far more basic part in human life—for instance, those involved in being black, or British, or blind. Whether feminism as a political movement will run out of steam is another (contingent) matter.

I write *as* a philosopher, because I believe that philosophy is an essential tool for both those who practice other disciplines (particularly psychology) and all human beings as such. We all have a life to lead, and we cannot lead it well without thinking philosophically about it. But, by the same token, I do not write only, or even chiefly, *for* philosophers. Indeed, I do not think we shall win many important victories in this or other areas until academics of various disciplines are much more willing and able to communicate, both with each other and with laymen, than seems now to be the case. I hope this book will at least further that particular cause.

I am grateful to numerous critics, in particular to Barbara Houston and Celia Dusoir for a good deal of tough-minded argument and to Nancy Swift for helping to keep at bay some of my own prejudices and fantasies in this area.

CONTENTS

PART I

SEXUALITY AND EROTICISM

1

SEX, PERVERSION, AND MORALITY

SEX

I begin with, perhaps, the most difficult topic of all—one that (so far as my reading goes) has not been adequately dealt with by analytic philosophers, despite some valiant and insightful attempts. My mention of "analytic philosophers" directs attention to the fact that our first job is to establish what we are talking about—the concept, the range of meaning, marked by terms such as 'sex,' 'sexual,' et cetera. It will be time enough later to enter into murkier waters that might be referred to by a phrase such as "the nature of sex." Whatever the nature and importance of overlaps between the strictly analytic task and other tasks, we have first to know what we mean.

One of the difficulties here is that the concept has arisen under a particular set of contingent conditions. I mean, briefly, the fact that for our species it is characteristically the case (not always) that a certain kind of desire is empirically linked, directly or indirectly, with certain independently identifiable features— the sexual or reproductive organs. I shall try to show shortly that this link is contingent and not conceptual, but it is certainly very strong. Indeed, there are two quite normal uses of the word 'sex' where the link is conceptual. First, we use 'sex' often simply as a criterion for distinguishing classes of creatures, including human beings, on strictly physical grounds, as when we talk of the male and female sex, "without discrimination of age or sex," and so forth. This use is like the German *Geschlecht* and reminds us of the Latin roots of 'sex': it refers to a particular class or set of creatures (unlike the German use of *Sex*, which

more or less represents the much trickier concept we shall be examining later).
Second, we talk of sexual encounters between animals, even of a fairly low
order. For example, scientists have spent much time on the sex life of the newt,
and, though we might doubt whether newts can be said to feel sexual desire (or
any desire), we do not hesitate to ascribe some kind of desire to, say, dogs. But
it is philosophically disputed whether—to put it far too grossly—"desire" in animals means the same as "desire"in human beings. We are not sure, empirically,
how far animals conceptualize, nor are we sure, philosophically, what (given that
they have no language) it would mean to say that they conceptualize, or what
difference it would make to our other beliefs about them. But it is, perhaps,
clear that with many animals (newts) the criteria of identification that govern
'sex' and 'sexual' are purely physical. Insofar as they extend beyond this, we include them in the much more baffling concept of sexuality as applied to man.

That the connection between what we mark by 'sex' in other senses than
the above and the (physically identifiable) sexual or reproductive organs is contingent and not conceptual may become more obvious in the following arguments. First, physical occurrences involving these organs are certainly not sufficient for the existence of sexuality (still in this wider, unexamined sense: it
might help at this point to mention phrases such as 'sexual desire,' 'sexual experience,' 'sexual feelings,' et cetera), since there are many cases where sexual
and reproductive organs are involved—for instance, in medical treatment and
surgical operations—but where we would have no temptation to talk of sexual
desire. One might even imagine a couple engaging in what, to all photograph-
able appearances, looked like a sexual encounter, even though they had no such
desire and regarded it as a kind of physical exercise. Some cases of actual encounters are not unlike this. Second, it is a little harder, but not too hard, to
show that the organs are not even necessary (harder, because of the characteristic connection mentioned just above). Sexual encounters can take place
between people who are sterile or who have had portions of their reproductive
organs removed. Many people enjoy sexual experiences without involving these
organs at all. It might be said that this is either 'perverted' or "incomplete"—
but, this has to be shown, and, meanwhile, there is no doubt that we apply the
terms 'sexual' to such cases. We can quite well imagine a state of affairs in which
the whole business of reproduction (for both sexes) was managed by an external
technology, as in Aldous Huxley's *Brave New World*. It would by no means follow, as it does not follow in Huxley's book, that the concept of sexuality dis-
appears—or even, I think, that it undergoes any essential change.

The problem about the connection with sexual organs, in the second
argument, is not really to do with *reproduction* at all. We find it hard to disso-
ciate sex from the sexual organs, not because they are the organs of reproduction but because they are the organs (or at least some of the bodily parts) related to sexual *pleasure*. There are features of sexual encounters, at least characteristically, such as "a relief from tension," "physical excitation," "penetration,"

"envelopment," even "closeness," that are usually tied to specific physical symptoms—what odiously clinical books on sex often call "pleasure zones." We overcome this difficulty by moving in the other direction; it is our concept of sexual pleasure—of the erotic, we might say—that is primary and dictates *which* physical features are not connected (except by proximity, as with the female clitoris) with the reproductive system at all. It is a contingent fact that the majority of human beings' sexual pleasure and desire seems to involve roughly identical parts of the body.

The Barbarella case is relevant here. In the film of that name, the heroine has an experience with another person (in an imaginary world): their palms are joined, and each appears to undergo symptoms of extreme and general physical arousal, followed by a relief of tension. If we were to argue about whether that was a sexual or erotic encounter, the argument would not turn on the fact that only the palms of their hands were involved. It might turn on whether the parties' physical symptoms showed the arousal to be sufficient, or sufficiently erotic (this might lead to tautology), to count as sexual; but that is a different matter. We might well be baffled by Andromedan desires in general, assuming that Andromedans have totally different bodies from ours and that they make their children externally, like artifacts. But, we would not *eo ipso* deny them the concept of sexuality altogether.

The Barbarella case may suggest that a necessary condition of sexuality, or the erotic, is *intensity* of feeling. But that seems wrong. There are, indeed, many cases of physical warmth and closeness—hugging, for instance—that are wholly nonsexual. But what makes them nonsexual is not their low temperature. One can have mild sexual desires and experience lukewarm eroticism. What does, perhaps, characterize sexuality is it *pervasiveness*. This is a point that Thomas Nagel seems to make in a well-known article;[1] but, I am not sure, because he connects it with other points that seem more disputable (particularly with the object of sexual desire being a person—see below). The point, anyway, is that there is something highly *generalized* about sexual desire. This is why it is pervasive. Whatever its object, sexual desire does not seek some particular feature of the object, as other desires do, but the object *per se*.

It is no objection to this to say that we do, very often, seek out sexual objects *because* of certain features that they possess (blonde hair or big muscles or whatever); nor to say that we often concentrate purely on certain *aspects* of objects (objects identifiable as such by other means) and screen out other aspects. For example, a man, following Ovid's advice in the *Amores*, might prefer to use certain sexual positions and not others with a woman, because she thus appears in a more attractive light and her physical deficiencies are hidden in those positions. Although all of this is true enough, the crucial point is that we cannot sensibly ask *what we want the object for*. The only answers we could give would be empty: "For pleasure," "To make love," "Because it seems desirable." There appears to be no particular *species boni* to sexual desire, as there is to ordinary appetites. We want food to taste good, chairs to be comfortable when we are tired, and so on, but we just want sexual objects to be "desirable." This tells us nothing—though it is easy to see how Freud and others come to write as if "sexual desire" meant simply "desire."

Freud's attitude is, in fact, not only forgivable but illuminating: for the difficulty of specifying any particular *species boni,* anything that one desires the sexual object *for,* seems insuperable. We might try a Platonic line (or one Platonic line), and say that the desire is for "beauty," if that is not too narrow an interpretation of the Greek *kalon* (as it almost certainly is). This line led Plato to say that the lover's proper object of desire—something we also need to examine—is the "Form of Beauty." But the trouble is, again, that this is too specific. It fits, perhaps, a characteristically male outlook or the outlook of the older of two homosexuals; but if a woman were to express her sexual desire for a man in such terms, 'beauty' and 'beautiful' would have extended their meaning too far to be of much use. It is true, of course, that sexual desire is (normally, though not always) sparked off by something in the *appearance* of the object, though even this idea has severe limits—voice tones, certainly erotic to many women (and men), are not part of appearance, unless we extend 'appearance' also, with equal uselessness. We may say that the object seems to us to represent the Good; but this, though not necessarily a pointless thing to say, in this context merely takes us back to the beginning.

Sexual desire is certainly linked to the object *qua* body, not qua the bearer of nonphysical properties. Again, it may be the case that nonphysical properties —intelligence, ancestry, social status, and many other things—*make* a person's body sexually desirable; but that is not to say that sexual desire is desire for these things. I say "the object *qua* body," not just "the body," because it is clear that in some cases (characteristically, though not necessarily) the object has to be a *living* body—that is, a body inhabited by a person. But that does not differentiate the desire for us. I may feel extreme desire to see, even to embrace, someone whom I deeply and intensely love (perhaps a child or a parent) without the least implication that this desire is sexual or erotic. This is because the person is not seen primarily in the physical mode (if the vagueness of that phrase may be excused for the time being). Whatever I do to him (her) physically is not, as it were, done for its own sake but as an expression or accidental symptom of some *other* kind of feeling—friendship, love, admiration, or whatever.

Sexual encounters exist for their own sakes, in this sense, which makes a great deal of sexual morality—not all of it—seem tiresome and irrelevant. Of course, nonsexual feelings may exist alongside of sexual ones, or they may be used, as by a certain kind of moralist, to license sexual ones. Nonsexual feelings may even, *pace* such a moralist, grow up after and as a result of sexual encounters. But love is a different concept from sexuality. The distinction is, admittedly, always difficult to draw in practice—not because the concepts overlap but because many people go in for both at once and many of the overt physical symptoms (hugs, kisses, embraces) are at least superficially similar. A particularly hard case would be: How do we distinguish Hamlet's embraces (if any) of Ophelia from his embraces of Horatio, a close friend? We have to say not that he felt *less* for Horatio, nor that his physical *expression* was less; not that sexual organs were involved in one case but not in the other; but, rather, that (though this is admittedly very general) he was not interested in Horatio's body as a general object of pervasive desire in the way that he was in Ophelia's. (If he had been, we should say that the relationship was genuinely homosexual.)

This involves a question about the object (or necessary object, if we can give sense to that phrase) of sexual desire. Nagel slithers a bit here but says that sexual desire "is a feeling about other persons" or "a particular individual." His statement seems plainly wrong: one can have sexual desires for animals. It could no doubt be argued even here (as it can more easily be argued in the case of shoe-fetishists, hair-fetishists, and the like) that the animals in some way represent people—that they constitute, as it were, the nearest that some men can approach to people as sex object. But this is a very different line of argument, which tries to say something (important) about the "natural" object of sexuality. The facts are that men can feel erotic desires about all sorts of things.

The plausibility and interest of this line of argument derive from certain facts, curiously neglected by most philosophers—briefly, that the first object of desire (or one of the first) for all human beings is, in fact, a person, namely, the mother or, as the psychologists would say, "mother-figure:" whatever person cares for, cuddles, and generally relates intimately to the infant. This leads naturally to the suggestion that sexual desire *ought*—whatever arguments we may give for this prescription—to have a person as its object or at least to the idea that a person is its "natural" object. Even this, however, is not straightforward. For at a very early stage of development, the infant has no concept of a person: the infant's world of desire, as psychologists describe it, is made up of what we might see as disconnected objects—in particular, perhaps, the mother's breast. So, if we are thinking about what is developmentally primal, persons are by no means the only or the best candidates. It is true, and no doubt fortunately true (for reasons I shall consider elsewhere), that the growing child fairly rapidly acquires some minimal concept of a person, at least as applied to its mother, and that it manages nevertheless to retain a high degree of sexual desire that is directed toward a person or people. Even here, however, many would say (not only Freud) that the gains that the child thus makes in coming to appreciate the existence of people, rather than disconnected objects like breasts, may be counterbalanced by losses in the amount of intensity of sexual desire, since (obviously) that desire has to transfer itself to a new object and may suffer loss in so doing.

This bears on our final question about sexuality: Is it inevitable, or inevitably important, for all men or for all rational creatures? Or is it some kind of option? Obviously, sexual *intercourse* or anything one might call sexual *experience* (falling short of full intercourse—I mean, some degree of acting out erotic feelings on or with the sexual object) is optional at least for adults. But that is just to say that one may *do* nothing about erotic feelings. The question is, Need one have them at all?

It seems inevitable that one will, for the following reasons. Any rational creature with a mind will necessarily be embodied and will necessarily perceive and sense the outside world. The mind, again inevitably, takes time to develop. Well before it is fully developed, it will have certain very general objects of desire, certain general 'goods'; and it will see these goods or objects chiefly, if not entirely, in the physical mode. What we have (very briefly) described here is what the infant feels (among other things) about its mother. It is not clear that the infant could feel any differently (the Freudian theory of infantile sexuality is a conceptual, not empirical, matter). This general, nonspecific desire for the object as such is what we mean by sexual or erotic desire.

Of course, the desire may become 'repressed', just as we can see in cases of *anorexia nervosa* where the desire for food (pretty basic, but more target-oriented than sexuality) becomes repressed; and/or it may become 'sublimated'— that is, directed into more specific channels, which themselves then take on a erotic or glamorous tinge. The terms 'repressed' and 'sublimated' need not carry the trappings of any particular empirical theory with them: they represent the only options for a desire—it keeps its original target, or changes the target, or goes underground. But the desire is still there, and inevitably there. Sexuality is not an option. That still, of course, leaves open the question of how far it is likely, or desirable, that erotic *feelings* be entertained in the conscious mind. The former is an empirical question (to which the answer will certainly vary from case to case), and the latter is so wide a question that it seems impossible to generalize. We may say, I suppose, that if pleasure-bestowing objects are available, and if undue trouble or damage is avoided, it is desirable both to entertain and to act on such feelings. We might think it worth adding that the background to sexuality, as described above, is likely to be so powerful (because it is so archetypal) that we should at least think twice before relegating too much eroticism to the unconscious—not, of course, that we usually have much choice in the matter. Further than that, at least in this very general way, we cannot go.

PERVERSION

I couple this apparently rather specialized topic with sex partly for illustrative purposes and partly because it provides a good lead into some of the problems in talking about sexual morality. Here, too, we need to be much more attentive to the meaning of the *words* 'perversion', 'perverse', et cetera. Thus, for instance, Nagel writes: "To return, finally, to the topic of perversion: I believe that various familiar deviations constitute truncated or incomplete versions of the complete configuration [of a full sexual encounter or experience] and may therefore be regarded as perversions of the central impulse." Later: "The concept of perversion . . . appears to involve the notion of an ideal or at least adequate sexuality that the perversions in some way fail to achieve," and "even if perverted sex is to that extent not so good as it might be, bad sex is generally better than none at all."[2] I quote this at length because it shows how easy it is even for highly competent philosophers to misjudge concepts. For it ought to be clear, even in advance of philosophical argument, that he is not talking about *perversion* at all: he is talking about inadequacy, which is quite different.

Perverse goes with such terms as 'wrongheaded', 'willfull', 'bloody-minded', 'pigheaded', 'unnatural', and 'against the grain'. A perverse way of doing something is not an inadequate way or a non-ideal way: it is a wrong-headed and, to put it rather enigmatically, an internally irrational way. In default of the appropriate technology, it would be perverse to try to build a house by starting with the roof. There are perverse ways of trying to translate a piece of Latin prose: not just stupid or wrong or inadequate ways but ways that (as it were) deliberately fly in the face of what the would-be translator knows and is trying to do. A perverse child is one who, at least characteristically, thwarts his own ends, not just (or perhaps not at all) those of other people.

We may also talk, though with more difficulty, about people being "perverted" or suffering from "a perversion." Some of the difficulty here is, of course, the too-hasty adoption of some rather simpleminded moral position (using 'moral' to refer, roughly, to the authoritarian morality common among many English speakers, particularly since Martin Luther, though the idea is far older). 'A perversion', in its most straightforward sense, need not involve such 'moral' ideas, except insofar as the term implies some deformity of the will—a perversion is not, though it may be analogous to, a physical deformity that a man cannot help. Quite commonly, things, not people, are said to be perverted: a translation may be a perversion (parody, caricature, distortion) of the original, or some statement, a perversion of the truth. There is still at root here the idea of a deliberate and irrational distortion: something that indicates that a man has behaved wrongheadedly, "against the natural grain."

How, in principle, could the concept marked by perverse get any kind of foothold in sexuality? First, we might ask whether sexual *desire* could be perverse. There seem to be difficulties about the idea of *any* desire being perverse *qua* desire. We may talk of a child perversely disobeying his parents because he desires to prove that he, too, has a will of his own or because he very much wants to hit his sister. Now it may, from an external standpoint, be *wrong* for him to disobey. It may be wrong for him to want to hit his sister, and though it can hardly be wrong for him to prove that he has a will of his own, he might go about proving it in a wrongheaded (perverse) fashion by hitting his sister. But this concept of perversion applied only to the last of these, which suggests that 'perverse' applies most naturally to behavior, not to desire at all. Desire may be in various ways wrong, misguided, inappropriate, inadequate, or inconvenient— but hardly perverse, or at least, not (to repeat) internally perverse. Of course, I may have an overriding desire, say, to build a house quickly and easily, so that my subdesire to start with the roof can be called 'perverse'. But that desire is not perverse per se.

This general point appears much stronger in the case of sexual desire, inasmuch as there is no specific *species boni,* no given or appropriate object of desire. Where there are such objects (in nonsexual desires), the term 'perverse' has a sort of foothold. There is (it might at least be thought) a proper *path* or direction for some desires, from which a man might (perversely) stray. If we thought, for instance, that ordinary food and drink were the natural objects of hunger, then we might—though in what seems to be a very loose sense—regard the desires of a man who only wanted highly spiced foods and very strong liquor as "perverted." They had, as it were, turned from the true path and showed some evidence that the man was going or had gone "against the grain" of his natural desires for food. I do not think this is very convincing even for other desires. In any case there appears to be no natural path for sexual desire—not, at least, in any very obvious and convincing sense of "natural." (Of course, we may make links between sex and, say, natural processes of reproduction, or natural law, or God's will, or something of that kind. Or we might give various external reasons why sexual desire is more satisfactorily directed toward some objects rather than others. But this is not good enough for talk of sexual perversion.)

Second, and much more plausibly, the word 'perverse' might apply to sexual *behavior:* to what a man does by way of following out or satisfying his desires. Here, the idea would have to be, in what I have taken to be the central sense of 'perverse', that the behavior was somehow self-defeating. The desire *per se* could not (logically) be perverse. His manner of executing it, however, might betray the existence of other desires that were not in place and that he wrongheadedly yields to, instead of taking the straight and natural path. For example, a man might find blonde hair sexually attractive, and there is no perversion in that: but suppose that, though available blondes abound, he insists on getting hold of brunettes and forcing them to wear blonde wigs in bed. That might reasonably seem to be a perverse way of getting what he wants, in a fairly obvious sense.

Even this is disputable—not because of any lack of clarity about what is to count as perverse but because it is nearly always unclear just what *content* a man's sexual desires have. Perhaps what the man really finds attractive are not just blondes but (so to speak) women who are compelled to be blondes. To take a more common case, suppose a man says he wants to seduce women but tends to tease them in a mock-aggressive kind of way, with the result that they regard as rude or boorish. We might say he was going about things in a perverse or wrong-headed way. That might be true—the concept does have application. It might alternatively be true, however, that what he really finds erotic are women who stand up to this sort of teasing and perhaps tease back, in which case his behavior is (other things being equal) wholly in order.

Third, we might talk of a perverted *use of* sexuality: something that we can distinguish from a sexuality that is itself perverted. Thus, if Nazi doctors in the concentration camps used medical science to conduct horrific experiments on Jews and others, this could fairly be described as a perverted use of medical science—the idea being, presumably, that medical science is attached to the aim or goal of curing people rather than of just observing how they behaved when in agony. This is different from the case where medical science is *internally* perverted (perhaps "corrupted" might be a better word; see Chapter 5)—for instance, where the kind of reasoning and the thought processes proper to such science were invaded by political or ideological pressures. In the former case, science is still science but has been put to improper use (as, some may think, with the making of atomic bombs or preparation for germ warfare); in the latter, the science itself is corrupted (as by astrology or witchcraft).

Sexuality seems to offer examples of the former kind: the glamorous spy, the gold-digging blonde, the man who uses his girl's sexual attachment to him in order to gain improper advantages from her. We can say here that sexuality is put to improper use: not because there is a "proper use" or goal to which we think sex must be attached (for instance, the procreation of children within marriage) but because *any* 'use'—that is, any *external* or extrinsic goal—would count as "improper." If we think that sexuality exists for its own sake (for fun, for pleasure), then any attempt to treat it as a means might be seen as wrong. A similar case, though perhaps requiring somewhat more moral severity, might be the use of food and drink to achieve economic advantage: if we thought that a shared dinner ought to be enjoyed by all the parties for its own sake, we might object to somebody arranging such a dinner (and behaving during it) so as to extract more export orders from his guests.

By the same token it is hard to see how sexuality offers any examples of the latter kind—that is, how it can be internally perverted in the way that science or any other rule-governed activity can be. Indeed, the whole of our discussion so far might seem to suggest that little or no *internal* evaluation of sex *per se* was logically possible: sexual activity is not an activity with standards or rules, and sex has no proper or 'given' object. This is, however, importantly erroneous in a number of ways. While we cannot answer the question What is sex for? in any way that brings internal standards of rationality into question—it is like other forms of play, one of the purest examples of an activity as an end in itself—the vacuous answer "For pleasure" does tell us something. For clearly such activities can be *vitiated* in various ways, and this is different from their simply being inadequate. We might even think that the 'natural' (nonrational) quality of these activities rendered them peculiarly liable at least to certain kinds of vitiation. We need to get much clearer about what these kinds are, before we can know whether terms like 'perverted', 'corrupt', 'distorted', et cetera, are in place.

The most important point here, perhaps—particularly in the prevailing philosophical and social climate of opinion—is that desires and the practices consequent upon them can be debased and shown to be such *without* reference to 'given' or 'proper' objects, which are naturalistically specified in a way independent of a particular person's satisfaction. Different things may suit different people: but a person's desires may be so vitiated that he cannot enjoy what suits him or even know what suits him. For instance, some sense can surely be attributed to saying that for certain people homosexuality is a 'natural' taste: for whatever reasons (possibly genetic), members of the same sex represent the sexual objects with whom they find the most basic erotic satisfaction of which their natures are capable. But some sense can also be made of the idea that for other people homosexuality is a second best—that their natural sex objects are heterosexual but that some intervening vitiation has made these objects difficult or impossible for them. Perhaps a particular man would find more satisfaction in women if only he were not unconsciously frightened of them or did not regard them as taboo; perhaps a particular woman would gain more erotic pleasure from men if only she did not see all men in the intolerable light in which she saw her father.

Sexuality is most commonly vitiated by *accompanying* beliefs or desires, which invade and make free erotic enjoyment difficult. Often, of course, we do not know whether a particular form of sexual expression is really "natural" or genuine or whether it has been vitiated (and I do not deny that there are philosophical problems as well as empirical problems about this, since the case history of every human being starts so early that it is hard to know what to count as "natural"). But often we can make reasonable guesses. It is barely possible that tortured women were a "natural" object for the Marquis de Sade's eroticism; but one would reasonably suspect, even before a detailed inspection of his case history, that his eroticism had been invaded, distorted, and overlaid by beliefs and desires of a different and exaggerated kind that had to do with control and power. Did he only feel *safe* when his sexual object was under total control and domination? Did he believe that it was somehow very difficult to have any *effect* upon women, so that only a very evident and exaggerated effect counted with him? These are the kinds of questions we should want to raise, because we at least recognize the possibility of vitiation.

Clearly, there are many possibilities of vitiation (I hope that subsequent chapters in this book will make some of them clearer) and it also seems clear that perversion will be one of them. That concept would apply when the person suffers (usually unconsciously) from accompanying mental states that willfully or pigheadedly thwart his own sexual enjoyment. Suppose that there is some (deeply buried) part of de Sade that would like him to enjoy women as erotic objects: then that would naturally—not because of any 'natural law' or moral theory but simply to enhance the enjoyment—lead him to value women, to enjoy being dependent as well as dominant on occasion, to find satisfaction when they expressed themselves in other ways than in screams of pain, and so forth. But other parts of him perversely (as we may now fairly say), fly in the face of all this—parts that deliberately make it all difficult. I do not imply that there is any correlation between perverted sexuality, in this sense, and what are commonly (for moralistic reasons) called "sexual perversions": it is quite possible that ordinary ("normal") heterosexual marriages would display on examination just as many, and as vitiating, fears, desires, and beliefs that accompany the sexuality as are displayed in the more outré forms of sexual behavior.

MORALITY

This is, of course, nothing like an adequate account even of perversion, let alone of other types of vitiation or (to use an even more general phrase) things that may go wrong with, or in, sexuality. But it may suggest something of the *kind* of way in which perversion and other concepts might gain a foothold—hence, something of the sort of philosophy required for this area. 'Moral philosophy' is probably too misleading a term for it, and 'philosophy of mind' does not seem quite right either; but the titles hardly matter. What matters, at least methodologically, is (to start with) an appreciation of the combined facts that sexuality is something that is, in important if obscure respects, *sui generis* and that the sexual area is one in which we do not (despite or because of its pervasiveness) know our way around, either conceptually or empirically. If we treat it as just another human activity ("form of life"), we run at once into trouble.

Characteristically, the kind of trouble we have arises because of a distinction commonly made (both in philosophy and in everyday thought) between questions involving negotiation with other people and a consideration of their interests, on the one hand, and questions (which may still be termed 'moral') about one's own ideals that do not, or need not, affect other people's interest in any significant way, on the other hand. I have discussed this later (Chapter 10), where it is of crucial importance. The trouble is that in most areas of life, and those not the least important, we confront both questions; it is not always wise to sever them too quickly. A good example of such severance—discussed more fully in Chapter 12—is R.M. Hare's essay on abortion, which he considers simply in the light of the golden rule or theory of universal prescription (aborting is harming a person-to-be's interests). Problems of abortion may be thought of as only tangential to problems of sexuality; but it seems clear even here that there are questions that might be asked concerning how a woman (or a man) ought to *feel* about the embryo or unborn child or what her interests in relation to the fetus really *consist* of. These are the difficult questions. They are not all to be dismissed as "matters of empirical fact," although the facts will vary from case to case. Answering them is very much a matter of getting at the roots of various concepts and practices.

Because of this severance, we tend to imagine either that sexual matters can be dealt with by some general moral theory (which can apply equally to other departments of life or that they are beyond the scope of reason and morality (in however extended a sense of that word)—that they are, as people say, "matters of taste." The former straitjackets sexuality, often into some improperly objectivist set of rules; the latter trivializes it. Behind both, perhaps, and behind the distinction just noted (between interpersonal morality and ideals), there may lurk an undue obsession with overt *action* with what people *do*—as opposed to how people feel and how they see themselves and the world. Yet, sexuality is a prime example of what various philosophers have been hammering home for several decades: that we cannot even describe—let alone explain or evaluate—what is being done in most cases, except in an extremely arid and meaningless way, unless we have some idea of what is going on in the heads and hearts of those concerned. Since what is going on may often be largely unconscious, we have to be still more careful.

It seems to me—and this is really the only thing I want to say about "sexual morality"—that if there is anything specifically to be so described, we can only make progress in the subject by a proper understanding of sexuality, together with some other concepts that seem inevitably to be connected with it (some, I hope nearly all, of these are dealt with later). This does not mean that "general moral theory", if that is a fair description for what (some) moral philosophers do, is not important in sexual matters. But otherwise, the case seems like medical and business ethics, though it matters that we speak of "ethics" rather than "morality" here, presumably because medicine and business are professions followed only by some men, whereas sexuality applies to men as such. Perhaps we could make better parallels by demarcating common features of human life—'the morality of personal relationships', 'the morality of work', and so on. Anyway, it seems that the right way forward in such cases would be—to begin with, at least—to examine the logical structure of the different areas themselves. Thus, some understanding of what work is (how to distinguish it from play, toil, rewarded activity, et cetera) and what its characteristic virtues are would be profitable: without this 'the morality of work' would be no more than a hasty application of some 'moral theory' to some (uncertainly grounded) cases of work—we should be told to apply the usual virtues, such as punctuality and respect for persons.

Finally, I should add—since Part II of this book is concerned with feminism and what might be called sexual politics—that it is crucially important to use the right kind of methodology even for these kinds of questions. It is at least possible that many people (not only feminists) have turned to politics partly out of a kind of unconscious despair: moral philosophy has served them so badly that all they can do is to adopt partisan positions of a political or quasi-political kind. (This might be one instance of a general truth about social movements in the present intellectual climate.) The truth is that we are a long way from having a clear answer to such questions as What is it to be a woman?; and if so, a good deal of the social concern—again, not only as expressed by feminists—is intellectually premature. We need to be able to tolerate much more doubt. This is easy to say and hard to do. Because sexuality is so fundamental and so pervasive that doubt about one's own or other people's sexuality (and all that goes with it) is among the most difficult things to tolerate. But we have to try.

NOTES

1. Thomas Nagel, "Sexual Perversion," in *Philosophy and Sex*, ed. Robert Baker and Frederick Elliston (Buffalo, N.Y.: Prometheus Books, 1975).
2. Ibid.

2

LOVE

Love is an impossibly large topic, and any connection it may have with
sexuality makes the topic still larger. Here I aim only to make some points that
have not (to my knowledge) been clarified elsewhere—points that are at least
among those particularly likely to worry us in practical personal relationships.
I have been much helped in this by W. Newton-Smith's article[1] (though he seems
to me to miss perhaps the most important issue). If I seem only to criticize it,
this is because he has given us something worth criticizing.

Prima facie, the word 'love' is a strong version of 'like'. One hates oysters,
does not like them much, is indifferent to them, likes them, likes them a lot, or
loves them. Not a few languages use a single verb (*aimer* in French, *amo* in Latin,
phileo in Greek), whatever other words they may have at their disposal. Love, as
some philosophers might have said in the recent past, involves a strong "pro" attitude. Like sexual desire, it does not appear to involve any particular *species
boni* (unless we say, rather emptily, that we see the love object as desirable, or
good, or lovable), nor does it involve any *belief* about the object. For that reason it seems unwise to classify love as an emotion along with other emotions
that (as is well-known)[2] do involve beliefs—pride, remorse, fear, and so forth. It
is, however, not a mood, like being depressed or (in a free-floating sort of way)
anxious, since it certainly has a *target* or object—there is something one loves.
Perhaps we could best classify it as a disposition. This at least fits in with our ex-
pectation that it will not—other things being equal—switch on and off easily, any
more than likes and dislikes switch on and off. Dispositions have some constancy.

16

We love (like, desire, feel attached to) objects under different descriptions: thus, I may love someone sexually or physically, Platonically, maternally, and so on. If influenced by some moral or metaphysical theory, we may be tempted to withdraw 'love' and substitute other terms: for instance, 'lust', if the attraction is exclusively or largely physical, or 'esteem' ('value', 'affection', et cetera) if the attraction is not physical enough. In general such temptation should be resisted, because we are too apt to import our own evaluations or some idea of what "true" ("real", et cetera) love is. Although, as discussed in Chapter 3, everyone brings some specific emotions and appraisals into his (her) sex life, nevertheless, sexuality may be disconnected from many of the things often associated (unnecessarily) with love. Such disconnections exist not only with sexual attraction but with other kinds of attraction or love also. They need not be seen as alarmingly schizophrenic.

Despite a long tradition of high-minded moralism (followed by Newton-Smith without, so far as I can see, any argument), there seems no doubt that the prime element in the concept is that of attraction and that whatever may be marked by 'affection', 'respect', and 'commitment' are not necessary features of it at all. This is plain where what I love is not a person: nobody expects me to feel affection toward oysters, or to respect them, or to be committed to them. It would be odd if the *concept* changed when applied to people as love objects. In fact, it does not. Just as, when we talk about "loving animals," we are apt to assimilate all cases to the case where one feels affection toward domestic pets and have to be reminded that one may love lions and tigers and bears precisely for their wildness; so we tend to assimilate all cases of human love to that of the virtuous home-seeking Odysseus and have to remember that one may (although admittedly it makes life difficult) love someone for whom one feels awe rather than affection, whom one knows to be (by any standards that have to do with "respect") worthless, and to whom one may not even wish to be "committed"— except in the tautologous sense that one's loving him/her "commits" one to that disposition. We do not deny that, for example, Edgar Allen Poe or the adorers of Greek Goddesses had their love objects, even though we may prefer the moral solidity of the ones favored by heroes and (more particularly) heroines in Jane Austen.

Is loving, then, just a strong version of liking? I think the answer to this is "Yes," if we are careful enough. Certainly with nonhuman objects it makes no sense to say, "I love X, but I do not like it". Why is it, if this is so, that we seem able to say this vis-à-vis people? Actually, such remarks—"I love him, but I do not like him"—are both uncommon and sophisticated. Normally, many people makes no such distinction: "Do you dig him?" (where 'dig' if this has not passed out of use by now perhaps stands somewhere between 'love' and 'like' and means something like "find desirable or attractive") is usually answered by a straight "Yes" or "No." The respondent may say, "Up to a point", but stays on that dimension and makes no distinctions. I suspect that in "I love him, but I do

not really like him" 'love' means something like "I am in love with" or "feel e-
rotic attraction toward." One might translate in some cases, "I find him desirable *qua* object of erotic attraction but not desirable *qua* companion," or something like that. 'Love', in English, can often slip into referring specifically (in giv-
en contexts) to "being in love with."

Because of this, there are some occasions on which 'love' seems to swallow
up 'like' and make questions of liking or disliking irrelevant. Suppose I love my
country or my home and am asked by a stranger, "Do you like England (Oxford,
your house on Chalfont Road)?" The effect of the questions will be to make me
step outside my strong disposition ("commitment") in favor of these entities
and assess them more objectively: as if I, too, were a stranger, deciding where it
would be most convenient, or nicest, to live and work. I could say, adopting this
(slightly forced) role: "Well, England is very unsatisfactory in some ways, Oxford is too crowded, my house is rather small, but"—changing roles—"you see,
I grew up there." We have to acknowledge a point here about "belonging,"
which I think nearer the mark than "commitment"—but I will leave this for the
present, because I want to come to it by another route. Normally, the question
"Do you like X?" where it is already known that the person loves X, does not
arise. We do not ask people if they *like* their children, except as a (rather odd)
way of eliciting the more detached response described above.

All this suggests that love is a *pathos* and not a *praxis,* something one finds
oneself feeling rather than deciding to do. That is certainly consistent with the
word 'like': one does not *decide* to like oysters. Love has (again, I suspect for
idealistic reasons) got muddled up with the ideas of "caring" and "concern,"
worth a brief comment here. 'Caring' either means something largely "behavioral" (that is, roughly, that one looks after, attends to, or meets the needs of
someone, as people care for the aged and the sick—but then this can be done
without love) or something like "holding dear or precious," which is nearer to
'love' but need not involve looking after or tending. It will be said perhaps, "But
if you love something, even in just your sense of 'thinking desirable' or 'finding
attractive,' will not that involve looking after and tending it?" Yes, but for *your*
sake, not for its', as a miser cares for his gold. So, too, with "concern"—one is
concerned in *one* sense for the beloved, in that one may want to possess or conquer her, and the rational man will no doubt be concerned that she should survive at least, in order that he may do these things. But one need not be altru-
istically concerned. Catullus was not, with Clodia/Lesbia; and it is difficult to
see how one can, in the required sense, "care for" or "be concerned about" the
stars, for instance, although clearly one may love them.

Newton-Smith's idea that "genuine concern or commitment cannot be ter-
minated simply by some revelation about or change in the object of that concern
or commitment"[3] just makes things worse. He says that we are not inclined to accept: "I was really concerned for her welfare so long as I thought she was pure

and innocent." I think we would, in fact, accept this: a member of the Communist Party can be genuinely concerned with the Party's welfare but (perhaps) abandons it altogether when it lends its support to what he regards as morally horrifying events (invading Hungary, for instance); so, too, with people. There is a muddle here between the causes or preconditions of 'genuine concern,' on the one hand, and what constitutes the concept, on the other. Whether love alters where it alteration finds (let alone bending with the remover to remove) depends on *what* is loved; of course, one can love a person "for his own sake" (that is, in such a way that changes or revelations about him can make no difference since they are simply irrelevant to a love with that object. If we stipulate that "genuine concern" is to mean this, very well; but that is not what it normally means. It is better to say (and this again leads toward our main problem) something like, "It was not *that person* whom you loved but (perhaps) your image of her as pure or innocent"—something, at any rate, about the *object* loved.

Is it a conceptual feature of love, as the author also claims[4], that the lover wants to be loved back? If loving people is essentially like loving things, obviously not. The case is hard to prove, simply because loving a person will *in fact* almost certainly involve wanting to be loved back. The lover is attracted to and desirous of the object and must, therefore, want to enjoy it (him, her) in some mode or other. The easiest way of ensuring this is to ensure that the object cooperates. Being loved back is a good form of cooperation (or is thought to be). But clearly the mode may vary; some like "worshipping from afar," not wanting to be loved back—not because (as in the *Little Dorrit* case quoted by the author) it would cause trouble to others but simply because they love in that particular mode—if Beatrice had come nearer to Dante, perhaps it would have spoiled things.

I approach now the main, problem, which is about what it is to love *Flossie* as opposed to *loving* Flossie—or, one might say, what it is to be loved "for oneself" or why (if this is true) another equally good, beautiful Flossie will not do as well as the original Flossie. Newton-Smith dismisses the worries here rather abruptly. The Stendhal theory (that we love only imaginary creations, not real people) will not do, because "we are not always mistaken about other persons. In many cases the beloved will in fact have some of the properties *on the basis of which* the lover loves" emphasis added; and the "psychoanalytic" view (that where A seems to love B, B is "a sort of stand-in in an elaborate fantasy") is "a misleading description of the case. For, it is towards B and not towards, say, his mother, that A performs the action appropriate in a context of love. Perhaps it is therefore best to say that A does love B while admitting the existence of *a causal connection* between his attitude towards his mother and his attitude towards B" (emphasis added).[5]

But these are straw men. It is a matter of interpreting the idea represented (by this author) by the words "on the basis of which," and the notion of "a causal connection" is not the only candidate. Suppose I claim to love Flossie, but it transpires that what I love about her consists solely of those properties that my mother possessed: why should we say that I love Flossie any more than that I love my mother, but, alas, my mother is not available whereas Flossie is? It is not a question of loving Flossie *because,* in any naively causal sense of the word, I loved my mother. There might be all sorts of reasons why, in this sense, I love Flossie. The worry is about just what I love or what it is about Flossie that I love. In more or less the same sort of way, if asked why one likes a certain piece of music or literature, one is not (at least not immediately) asked for or expected to produce a causal story: one is being asked *what it is about* the piece that one likes—its *species boni.* When one has given that answer, a further (causal) question might be raised about why that particular *species* happens to move the speaker, but this is a different question.

The example from music may make things more rather than less mysterious; but presumably there will be *things about* a piece of music for which one likes it, just as (to take simpler cases) one may like objects just because they possess certain properties. I do not like this particular hammer: anything that knocks nails in as well will do as well. It sounds odd to say that any other piece of music that has the properties of this one will do as well, but that may only be because pieces of music are all significantly different and in fact have very different properties—our desires in relation to them are much more complex than our desires about hammers. But we must, to repeat, like the piece *qua* something or other; so that, in principle, another piece *would* do as well. Or if not, why not?

Some people might be content to rely on the complexity of human beings, which is no doubt greater even than that of music. But this is not really the complaint or not the only complaint. When people want to be loved for themselves, they do not want to allow the idea of any substitutes, even in principle. "You don't love me for myself alone but only for my yellow hair, my blue eyes, my . . ." etc. etc. remains a complaint, even if the number of etceteras makes it unlikely that a substitute will be found. If we took what Newton-Smith represents as the "psychoanalytic theory," all we could do would be to count ourselves fortunate that B's qualities are sufficiently coextensive with A's mother to make life tolerable for B. "Only God, my dear, can love you for yourself alone and not your yellow hair."

Nor is the problem solved by interpreting such complaints as exhausted if A loves B for what B regards as central to "herself." Certainly this can be meant: if B sees herself not primarily as the possesor of yellow hair but of, say, a profound soul and a brilliant intellect, she may be apt to say that A_1 does not love her "for herself"; but then, alas, A_2 deserts her for B_2, who possesses a still deeper soul and a still more brilliant intellect. It is just at this point that, pitying B_1, we want to talk about "commitment." The difficulty is to make any sense of this without either forcing it onto the concept of love or just moralizing.

It is really a problem about the merits of the particular as against the universal or the Form. Plato reasoned (at least in the *Symposium*) along the following lines: a man loves X (a beautiful boy, or whatever); now, what we should say is that he loves the physical beauty of X—there must be something *about* X that calls forth the love, and this seems to be it; he may find a superior beauty in the soul of X, and love X for that, but that, too, means that what he *really* loves is—and will be, once he gets the point and puts in enough practice—the Form of Beauty, the Beautiful, part of the Form of the Good. This is a very popular idea (partly because Plato invented it). God, for instance, is used as some kind of ultimate or all-inclusive object of all loves, because God contains everything desirable (*ex hypothesi*), and, obviously, one cannot love anything undesirable, so really one can only love God (and his manifestations, but only qua manifestations). Lovers commonly say that their beloved represents, or encapsulates, or in some way stands for all that is beautiful—she is like a red, red rose, or is clad in the beauty of a thousand stars, or all that is best of dark and light meet in her aspect and her eyes. Now, why should not the girl get huffy over this and say: "Ho, I see it is really roses and stars and dark and light you love. I'm just a stand-in—you do not love me for myself at all"?

I think she could reasonably get huffy, if that was all there was to love—of course, not too huffy, since it is flattering even to be a stand-in to the divine Forms (rather like understudying Laurence Olivier), and (so far) it appears that none of us can do any better anyway—we are all poor particulars. Something is basically missing here—it is the idea of *belonging*. I love my mangy, scruffy, bad-tempered cat because she is *my* cat: plainly not because she instantiates any desirable Forms—or, at least, not those Forms normally on the preferred short list. Can other Forms apply? That is, is something's being mine (assuming we can make any sense of this) a good reason, or any kind of reason, for loving something?

It is certainly *some* sort of reason, because we see it operate frequently. Parents love their children because they are theirs (extensions of themselves, Aristotle suggests—there is the germ of a psychological theory there), and I love my cat, country, house, et cetera, because they are mine. The attraction, of course, is that this makes them in principle irreplaceable. At least I have to grieve over losing my house (however awful it was, I loved it), and perhaps build a similar relationship with another house; I cannot just replace it without loss. In many, perhaps most, complaints of the form, "You don't love me," there is an idiosyncratic demand: me, not *qua* the bearer of certain properties but (mysteriously) me *qua* me. The worry here, and perhaps Plato's bewitchment, consists in the feeling that we have to *justify* love or at least to justify it in a certain kind of (external) way—to show that the object is *worth* loving. But if we adhere too closely to this, then the object is not loved *per se* but only *qua* the bearer of properties.

The idea of justifying our attachment to particulars seems rather strange: could we imagine human beings *not* becoming attached in this way? No doubt questions can be raised about what particulars we *ought* to become attached to: indeed, they are in and out of our minds much of the time (whom should we marry, where shall we live, et cetera). We can put those questions in the form: "To what objects should we become 'committed'?"; but that makes it sound like an act of will. It is only an act of will inasmuch as in certain circumstances one can make a particular decision to put oneself in a certain setting whereby one may (one hopes) *become* so attached—deciding to buy the house or marry the girl. Becoming attached takes time more than anything to be called "will power." If it does not happen, there may still be things one can do about it; for example, one may go to a psychoanalyst, hoping to learn to be more attached to one's wife or job. (The whole distinction between what is and is not "under the control of the will" is quite unsatisfactory: philosophers have tended to think that only what can be *immediately* done by choice is 'under the control of the will'. But we can, slowly, change lots of other things—even our desires.)

Certainly the question can be raised, Is it good to become attached in this way? Or, if it is inevitable, we can ask why it is. Of course, it is not inevitable with respect to all objects: "Breathes there the man with soul so dead that never to himself hath said 'This is my own, my native land [Flossie, cat, house, et cetera] ?'" has to be answered in detail—not everyone loves all categories of things. The satisfaction of the desire for what is (in no "possessive" sense) one's own is considerable and more rewarding than the other aspects of love, which might otherwise represent a sort of constant pursuit of the Good that one never quite catches up with. In this aspect one can be home and dry. (The concept of a home is one good example.)

There is, it might be thought, nothing very *erotic* about this aspect of love (though it is worth noting that there is nothing very "altruistic" about it either). But I think this would be a mistake, mostly made by those who try to capture some Form—or, we might more realistically say, recapture some parental image of the desirable—by a series of sexual adventures. Bodies, too, particularly when inhabited by people, are particulars that can be loved qua particulars. It is naturally often difficult to determine whether some lovable features—the way a person's hair curls, or whtever—are loved because they represent some Form or image, or because they become familiar; the two are distinct, even though one would not *start to become* attached to the particular if it did not instantiate some form.

Is this necessarily a part of the *concept* of love? Is it not just a certain kind of love or a contingent feature that may go along with love, certainly convenient and rewarding but not of the essence? The answer is that it is not, *sans phrase*, part of the concept of love but part of the concept of loving a particular person or object. Finding *Flossie* (the cat, the Pleiades, Greece) desirable and enjoyable is, strictly, only possible if these objects are not replaceable, and this means attachment to them as particulars. Of course, as Aristotle might say, we *call* it love when there is no apparent attachment, but we can always raise the question of whether the object is what it is supposed to be. This does not mean that, for instance, a man might not love a class of people in a certain mode—tall willowy blondes; then his girl friend could not say that he does not love anything, but she can say, "You do not love *me*, any tall willowy blonde would do as well." Classes can be particulars ("Women? I love 'em all!"), though certain particular classes can be inconvenient for forming attachments to in the way described earlier.

In practice, our search for Forms or parental images, for qualities rather than particulars, is inevitable and necessary—that is to say, we cannot just love *anything*. We love things because there is something about them. But we have to negotiate that aspect of love alongside of the attachment aspect: to find the exciting, erotic, adventurous, thrilling, et cetera, *in* the familiar. Proverbs such as "Absence makes the heart grow fonder" and "Familiarity breeds contempt" testify to the difficulty of doing this: to some extent, no doubt *semper abest quod avemus*. Some such negotiation is the only alternative to being either irretrievably nomadic or bored.

NOTES

1. W. Newton-Smith, "A Conceptual Investigation of Love," in *Philosophy and Personal Relationships*, ed. Alan Montefiore (Montreal: McGill, Queen's University Press, 1973).

2. See John Wilson, *Education in Religion and the Emotions* (London: Heinemann, 1971), with references to Kenny and Peters.

3. Newton-Smith, "Conceptual Investigation of Love," p. 132.

4. Ibid., p. 126.

5. Ibid., pp. 125-26.

3

LOVE-OBJECTS AND THE BODY

The difficulty here, as so often, is to distinguish between the conceptual, the empirical, and the evaluative ('moral', in a broad sense, though this often includes one's own tendency to upgrade one's preferred pictures into some kind of general use). These categories are not as distinct as they seem. Although conceptual *arguments* can be distinguished from empirical ones, it is often hard to say what status the resulting beliefs have; and the "evaluative" is not really a special field in itself—conclusions here emerge chiefly from the conceptual and the empirical. All of this rests under an enormous weight of philosophical literature—I have said a little about some of the points elsewhere.[1] I mention the difficulties here simply to put the reader on his guard.

The problems here might be approached by this (very vague) question: Granted that sexual desire is desire for some object *per se*, granted that we ourselves inhabit (or are partly constituted by) bodies, and granted that we are brought up as children by embodied people, can anything be said about sexual encounters? There are two conceptual points that may guide us here: a point about why sexual experience must be psychologically important for us and a point about why emotions (not just sensual feelings) inevitably get attached to it.

The first point has been discussed philosophically elsewhere but chiefly from a social angle: the suggestion is, roughly, that no society could regard experiences and organs concerned with reproducing its own species as unimportant. That is, perhaps (only perhaps—a society might sincerely believe that it ought simply to die out), generally true. But, as I have tried to show earlier, there is no conceptual link between sex and reproduction. The question is rather, Why should we regard sex as "special"? Why should we (as we nearly all do) make such a fuss about it? Why should we not say that the fuss is simply due to generations of puritans or other kinds of people who have *thought* it to be "special" when it was not? Why should it not simply be regarded as another appetite—admittedly, without any specific object or *species boni*—just a highly generalized form of pleasure (perhaps rather like resting, or taking a warm bath, or the sort of enjoyment one may have in one's own body as a whole, when functioning properly)? Why, for instance, could we not regard rape as not different in principle from forcibly pushing a stick into someone's mouth?

To take the last question: we feel tempted to say that rape involves more *intimate* parts of the body, that it invades *privacy* more, or that it is in some way more *disruptive*. But why are these parts of the body more intimate or private? There is a weaker and a stronger reason here. The weaker reason is that there is a quite straightforward sense in which the *penetration* of a person's body *is* more invasive or disruptive than some treatment that does not involve penetration. Having something shoved down one's throat, for instance, may be less painful than (say) being beaten but not less invasive. The stronger reason is that sexual features of the body are, precisely, those parts that are most sensitive to *pleasure*: this is a conceptual point, because the sex organs are defined by sexual pleasure, not the other way around (if Martians get their biggest erotic thrills by interlocking fingers and toes, those would be their sex organs). Because of this, these organs will inevitably be seen as "special" by their owners and other people. Exactly how they see them may vary, but it is hard to see how they could not grow up some concept of privacy about them, just because they are unusually sensitive and give unusual possibilities of eroticism.

It may often be uncertain whether the former or the latter reason, or both, operates in a particular case. When T. E. Lawrence was raped by the Turks, for instance, it is an open question whether he saw this as unpleasant just because it involved penetration and/or because it involved interference with a semisexual organ, an "erotic zone." This would depend on how Lawrence himself felt about the organ in question (of course, he may even have enjoyed it and not counted it as "interference"). I describe the second reason as "stronger" only because it is more specifically allied to *sexuality*. When girls or children are "interfered with," to use the language of the police court, there is often no question of penetration; but privacy is invaded because certain parts of their body (breasts, or whatever) are "special"—that is, especially erotic and sensitive and, therefore, to be specially defended against interference, used or enjoyed only when the owner licenses it. I raise the Lawrence case because (as is well known) the organs of excretion do, in fact, give rise to erotic impulses in many adults. It is not only—not even primarily—either a matter of "social conditioning" (children being told that these things are "dirty") or the mere proximity of excretion to genitalia (eroticism, as guilt, acquired by association), it is, again, because the functioning of these organs can hardly help being a major issue in the early life of any child (whether or not 'toilet-trained'), inasmuch as they play a large part as representing some very salient things that he *does* and *feels*.

The kind of privacy involved in sexuality (there are other kinds, mostly simpler and concerned merely with private property and privately controlled space, which might be desired for much more "unemotional" reasons) leads to an inevitable ambivalence. These organs or areas are "special," highlighted as being unique purveyors of pleasure (both for oneself and for others) and under special guard for the same reason—they may be hurt or damaged, or they may be aroused against or independently of one's will. We recognize that we are, in this way, subjugated to parts of our bodies: in principle (and in practice) we can hold each other down and simply make each other feel certain strong sensations—quite apart from the possibility of actual damage. Hence, all societies both highlight and protect. If one were to raise the Freudian question whether, for example, women's clothes were designed to emphasize female sexuality or to conceal and guard it, it would be difficult to give a straight answer—not that the concepts are not distinct but that they arise side by side from a common source.

I turn now to the second point. So far as the concept marked by *sex* goes, there is no reason why sexual desire should not be felt for any object, nor is such desire tied to any particular emotion (else it would have a *species boni*). But it will inevitably be tied to some emotions, perhaps many. This is because, to put it briefly, we are not animals—and in saying that I do not imply anything 'moralistic'. The point is that we are, willy-nilly, conceptualizing creatures; so that, unless we are asleep or in a state of total mental vacancy, we are more or less bound to *attach* some *species boni* to the object (often unconsciously—this makes no difference). We find the object generally desirable *because* it has certain features: we see it *as* beautiful, tender, fresh, queenly, strong, dainty, or whatever. Our style of behavior toward it is also involved: instead of simply seeing it as something we want to merge with or (in a highly general sense) "possess," we see it perhaps as something we want to arouse, conquer or be conquered by, protect and cuddle, strip naked, be very close and secure with, exercise power over, and so forth.

It is a further conceptual point (or perhaps part of the same one) that, because we are reared as infants and children by *people*—and if we were not, we would not grow to be people ourselves—many of these emotions, together with the first experiences of physical pleasures, will necessarily be related to persons or, at least, to our perceptions of persons. This is, from the strictly logical viewpoint, a much looser kind of truth (though empirically very important), because the degree to which and the way in which one's emotions and sensations are person-related may vary: I claim here only that the (inevitable) case history of any child must enforce some degree of such relationship. Consider the following example: if our sex objects are, *au fond,* just certain physical objects—breasts, for instance—why will it not do for a man to enjoy merely an inflatable, rubber life-size doll with breasts? Well, perhaps for some men it *will* do (though one might suspect that a real woman would better, if only some psychological difficulty did not get in the way); but most men would want to say something like, "It's not alive enough." "Very well, what's missing?" "I want to caress the breasts and make the nipples erect." "OK, we can build that into the doll." "Ah, but I want to hear the tender-taken breath, the sighs and groans, and have the doll move, and say things, and so on." Maybe we can build this into the doll, but we clearly move nearer and nearer to building a person.

To put this more simply: the boy wants his mother (or the girl her father, or whatever persons are involved on either side for either) not just *qua* object. Wanting her *qua* object defines, conceptually, the specifically *sexual* nature of his desire; but *pari passu* with that, and inextricably linked with it, so that in practice it is virtually impossible to sever the two, are desires for other than merely physical responses. He wants perhaps to make an *impact* on her as a person (only necrophiliacs omit this) and her to make an impact on him: to seduce, surprise, perhaps frighten a little, or conquer and, perhaps also, to be reassured, forgiven, conquered in turn. Notions like aggression and passivity can hardly avoid entering into this—and there may be even more specific notions, such as pride (in one's performance or body), the desire to tease, protectiveness, and many others. These emotions do not totally disappear as the child grows; they may often go underground (which is one reason why it is so hard to say why one's sexual tastes are what they are—the emotional *species boni* is unconscious), but in adult sexual relationships they inevitably play a very large part. This remains true even if one's preferred sex object is not a person: one will, inevitably, invest the object with something like personal qualities. (It is for many people very difficult *just* to masturbate: they masturbate in the grip of some *species*, perhaps with a story or fantasy attached. At a minimum there is the idea of someone *doing* something to, or with, or for them.)

We see then that, in this fairly minimal sense, the idea of *personal involvement* is inevitable. At this point it is tempting to start talking about love—but prematurely. If the involvement of a sadist with a masochist is a case of love, clearly "love" is going to be a useless term for us here, at least without prior examination. What we can say, and have in effect said, is that people bring themselves—their emotions—into sexual encounters. What now, we might profitably ask, becomes of the notion of a "sex object"? Is it reasonable to see people as sex objects? Only as sex objects (something much objected to by feminists)?

There are various wrong answers here, which we need to get clear about. Plainly, you can love someone without viewing him erotically, and vice versa: whatever may be said in favor of love having something to do with sex, there seems to be no internal connection. It is not *perverted* to engage in sex without love, nor is it in any *obvious* way wrong or even "inadequate" (inadequate for what, we might ask—plainly not inadequate for sexual pleasure). On the other hand, what could be *meant* by seeing someone "only as a sex object"? If that were to be interpreted (wrongly) to mean "only as a (physical) object for sexual pleasure," we could make little sense of it. What we have said above suggests that "pure" (animallike) sexual pleasure is impossible for conceptualizing creatures like men—some emotion, some person-relatedness, inevitably enters. So it seems that feminists object to the logically impossible.

To see someone as a sex object is to see him (her) as an attractive target for sexual desire, inevitably involving certain emotions bound up with that desire. This in itself must be unobjectionable, since it is no more than a description of any sexual encounter. To see him (her) *only* as a sex object means, presumably, that the range of the viewer's interests, emotions, and desires is limited in some way. It is not limited in the sense that, *a priori*, only certain feelings and emotions can be specified as "sexual," for more or less any emotions may enter into sex, but in the sense that the viewer is only interested in those of his emotions and feelings that are, in the way described earlier, bound up with sexual desire. For example, a man may be interested in a woman only as providing him with a suitable target for whatever feelings are marked by "conquest" or "aggression"—these feelings being cashed out in physical contact and pleasure—or a woman in a man only *qua* a person object she can feel close to, or have safe inside her, under similar conditions.

Offhand, there does not seem anything particularly wrong with this either—certainly nothing that can be demonstrated by such terms as 'using people', 'not respecting persons', 'loveless', and the like. For the facts are, as we know very well, that in *this* sense we 'use' people all the time: this is simply to say that we nearly always (perhaps, again, inevitably, always) limit the range of our interests and emotions according to the mode in which, or the purpose for which, we are relating to them. We 'use' people as friends, lovers, tennis partners, and so forth. Of course, there is an overriding point about other people's interests or options: we have to treat them as equals, do deals with them, not be egocentric, prescribe universally, or however we care to put the point. This applies to all relationships. Who "uses" whom, in any derogatory sense of that word, must be a function of whether justice is done: if the person being "used" likes it, then he (she) is not, in the required sense, being "used."

Again, it might be thought that there is something inadequate, if not actually wrong, in limiting one's interests in this way. This, too, seems mistaken: a friend is not inadequate if he is not also a lover; and relationships are not inadequate just because we do not play golf together as well. There is a very strong idea, when it comes to sexuality, that the limits are somehow set for us, perhaps by God or nature: that it is somehow wrong or (if we dislike moral language) inadequate if, say, the man does not care two pins about the woman's intelligence, or the woman has no interest at all in whether the man loves her or not. If there is anything in that idea, it needs arguing for.

We can do a little better by some such terms as 'impoverished' (with some such opposite as 'rich'); for it is clearly true that the more, and stronger, emotions are satisfied in a sexual encounter, or a series of such encounters, the more satisfactory they will be, a conceptual truth if anything is. Here, too, we must be careful. Suppose a man puts most of his aggression into his work and little into his sex life: apart from any question of other people's interests, why should we say that his sex life is 'impoverished'? Why should we say that it is a *pity* that he does not get more out of it? It would only be a pity if he could not satisfy his aggression elsewhere. 'Impoverished' suggests, once again, some kind of *standard* against which we measure what ought and ought not to go into sex; it is hard to see where such a standard could come from. Some people like just stroking each other; others like a whole range of activities, a whole set of "games," a whole gamut of emotions. What can we say except "Good luck" to all of them?

I think something more can be said about this, but here in particular we have to watch the status of our arguments carefully. What makes the highly generalized idea of universal prescriptivity, or "treating others as equals," or "giving equal weight to other people's interests" so weak a tool here is that, in this area above almost any other, people do not *know* what their interests are. We may talk glibly about making deals ("No strings, we are both adults, agreed?"), but we constantly deceive ourselves in relation to what we want and what other people can (or will) give us. The real trouble with many, perhaps most, sexual encounters is not that they are perverse, morally wrong (either through not treating people as equals or in some other, more mysterious way), or just "inadequate" or 'impoverished' but rather that they are *mismatching*. The (usually unconscious) expectations of the two parties do not *fit*. This is perhaps a fairly obvious (though important) suggestion that we should all search our souls, or have them searched by a psychoanalyst, in an endeavor both to find out what we do really expect from or 'put into' our sexual desires and perhaps to change the ingredients if inconvenient. It may also suggest certain other general points.

The first of these wears traditional clothes but is none the worse for that. What we have noticed about sex difference implies that the *kind* of emotions or general feelings 'put into' sexuality will vary as between men and women. It is hard to describe these, partly because the language is shot through with ambiguity. However, if we accept something like the active/passive or initiator/respondent distinction that I argue for later (see Chapter 8), we can also accept that it will be a preponderantly (not uniquely) male interest to import feelings concerned with conquest and aggression and a preponderantly female interest to import those concerned with being a desirable and responsive object. The man will naturally want to seduce, strip, overcome, arouse, and in general *affect* the woman: if he is very passionate (or very uncertain) about this, he may be particularly gratified by moans, involuntary squirms, pleas for mercy, and so forth. The woman will naturally want to be seen as a potent person object, not so much potent in activity but potent in eliciting activity; she also wants to feel secure, be cherished, and made to feel complete (the man, as it were, permanently inside her), not deceived or abandoned or betrayed. She may require a background of (not specifically sexual) trust or semipermanence.

I do no more here than generalize, not only from the many "books about sex" printed today but from the tradition of almost all societies and ages. It is perhaps worth adding swiftly that, of course, individuals vary on these and other dimensions; that I have highlighted the differences in feeling—many feelings will be identical to both sexes; that, although this may be the "basic natures" of the two sexes, many of us do not accept our basic natures in certain respects (or even in general), so that our "surface" needs and options may be completely contrary to them; and that (perhaps most important of all in this context) there is nothing wrong, or even regrettable, in the existence of these differences. Wise and loving partners will presumably so arrange things that the interests of each are catered for—if necessary, in turn. It is a common fantasy to suppose that there is some kind of "ideal" sexual activity, in which all the emotions and desires of both partners are gratified completely in the same way at the same time. Sexual encounters involve a relationship between *two different* people.

The second point, about which I feel much more uncertain, has to do with the ideal of monogamy: I mean, in this context, the ideal desirability of limiting one's sexual encounters to some one person. There are plenty of *ad hoc* arguments for this (valid or not): the need to keep a family together, the general convenience of having one's sexual gratification permanently available, the avoidance of various kinds of trouble and instability, and the institutionalization of (what may be seen as inevitable features) possessiveness and jealousy. I do not dismiss these, but (as so often) they appear to be mostly—perhaps not the last— external or extrinsic arguments, not arguments designed to enhance sexuality itself. This is, presumably, why nowadays they are not commonly attended to: people want more sexual satisfaction and think that they have at least the chance of it if they are not monogamously restricted.

Other less *ad hoc* arguments might be advanced. It might be said, not without plausibility, that the the degree of *trust* required not just to enjoy sexuality but to explore our sexual feelings is unlikely to be gained in promiscuous relationships: it takes time and some degree of shared life outside sexuality itself. Promiscuity, it might be said, is like having many friends but no close friends— rather like knowing a little about many academic subjects but nothing much about one. Specialization adds whole new dimensions to friendship as it does to learning. It might even be possible to argue that, since in practice a person's earliest love object is some *one person* (mother, father, or whoever), it goes against the psychological grain to hedge one's bets: the promiscuous person, as it were, is constantly in search for some one partner with whom he can satisfactorily identify his original love object.

These arguments, too, are not absurd, but one might more plausibly rely on a rather different kind of argument, at which some of the above do no more than hint. It involves a concept used by literary critics, commonly marked by "multivalency." The idea is that a work of art is to be preferred if it appeals on different levels and in different aspects rather than just in some one mode: our relationship to it is more rewarding, inasmuch as it is "richer" or "has more in it." A similar, perhaps better, example would be the idea of one's native land: not many people would want to argue that it is better to be a stateless person, albeit with knowledge and experience of many countries, than a person who has a particular love and deep understanding for some one country.

Suppose we take an example of a sexual feeling that might seem difficult to fit into this new picture—for instance, the man's desire for adventure and conquest. It could be said that if he wants to adventure into interesting or *rich* territory, or conquer something *worthwhile*, he will do better to direct his sexual attentions to a woman he knows rather than to a number of women whom he does not. This may sound odd, because "adventure" does not seem to fit with what is already known nor 'conquest' with what has already been conquered, simply shows the limits of territorial analogies. Just as, if his mind is properly in order, it will be more rewarding for him to conquer a real woman than a rubber doll (even if the doll is programmed to resist for a bit)—because there is "more to" a real woman—so it will be more rewarding for him to move more fully into the heart of a woman whom he knows well.

It seems to me that, in principle at least, there is nothing *deficient* in monogamy: people are in a very real sense infinitely mysterious, contain all human emotions in infinitely flexible forms, and are capable of infinite learning and enjoyment from each other. What happens, of course, is that we find it (often) insuperably *difficult*. Flossie is a nice girl and making love to her is fun, but Melisande is more mysterious and exciting; there is just no way (it seems) that I can turn Flossie into Melisande. John is a nice chap, always considerate and quite the gentleman, and certainly I feel safe with him: but Ramon, though undoubtedly a swine, is much more thrilling. Or—if we are the classical Greeks—we make a convenient split (convient for the male, that is, or so the males thought) between the wife at home and the cultivated courtesan.

To say that there is something "wrong with" splitting in this way is not to suggest that we should restrain ourselves by an act of will—even if we could. These are (dissociated) parts of our natural desires, and—other things being equal—why should we not satisfy them? Indeed, it is psychologically important that we should not only satisfy them but come to understand what they are, which requires some experience. In practice, we have to do the best we can with the equipment we have, and even trying to change it is a very long job. This is why, at best, we can regard monogamy as an 'ideal': something perhaps to be worked toward, but not at the cost of denying what we *now* need. The mistake of monism is to achieve the One only at the cost of denying or disregarding certain crucial constituents: as the Jews (in contrast to the Greeks) achieved the idea of one God only at the cost of removing from his nature many of life's aspects that we might find admirable or even worshipful (sexual enjoyment being one). In practice, all we can perhaps say is that we should enjoy ourselves, avoid hurting other people, and *learn what we are really like*. This, goodness knows, is difficult enough.

NOTES

1. John Wilson, *A Preface to the Philosophy of Education* (London: Routledge & Kegan Paul, 1979).

4

AGGRESSION

Sexual desire brings other things with it. Among these are what may most properly or conveniently be called *emotions*—that is, feelings that involve specific beliefs. For instance, one may see the sexual object as dangerous and be frightened of it, or as peculiarly admirable and be proud of it, or as having been spoiled by one and hence feel guilty about it. Although these emotions are complicated enough, the existence of false beliefs at least offers a foothold for rationality and (self-) education: the beliefs, if not hopelessly deep below the level of conscious retrieval, can be made to surface and can be inspected for their correctness and appropriateness. Much more difficult to deal with is an item (or set of items) that is hard even to classify (mood? disposition? attitude?) but for which the term "aggression" might not be, as a starter, too misleading.

One reason why it seems necessary to say something about "aggression" is that in *some* sense it seems inevitable to enter into, or constitute part of, sexuality. I do not mean that males characteristically "get hold of" and "invade" or "penetrate" females; feminists would hold that the phenomena here could be equally well described by saying that females 'stimulated' and then 'envelop' or 'possess' males (or something of that sort). I mean, rather, that some kind of forceful initiative or striving toward the object enters into sexual desire—indeed, one might say, into all desire (this is what we mean by the word 'desire'). The stronger the desire, the stronger the trying-to-get behavior, and such behavior might be called "aggressive."

But to say this, as we have just seen, is to do no more than note the con-

33

nection between desiring and trying to get: if 'aggression' refers only to that, it is uninteresting and certainly not specifically sexual. What else might it mean? The trouble is that 'aggressive' and 'aggression' are nowadays almost terms of art, much used by psychologists and other empirical scientists, with a heavy spillover into "normal usage" (rather like 'role', 'heurotic', and others). There seem to be at least the following three options:

1. Forcefulness. We commonly speak of someone tackling, say, a problem "aggressively," meaning no more than "forcefully." This is normally considered a good thing where the activity calls for a certain kind of effort and subjugation of the material; a bad thing, or perhaps rather an irrelevant thing, when the activity is not of that sort. It is in order to display forcefulness in playing football, even perhaps in an argument. It would be much odder to speak of the desirability of aggression in novel writing, although forcefulness is required (we like forceful writing), the need for it is not so much to the fore—good novelists need things like sensitivity as much or more. It would be impossible to speak of a forceful or aggressive mediator or prayer or nurse—these activities require other virtues. It seems very hard to specify this difference exactly: I have said "a certain kind of effort and subjugation," but what kind? We might say that in the former activities the person need not *respect* or *respond to* the materials of the activities so much, whereas in the latter most of the task might precisely consist of respecting and responding. Thus, in being an aggressive businessman or football player I have to keep certain rules, but otherwise I simply do my damnedest to gain certain very specific ends—a goal or a monopoly—and can proceed in a wholly tough-minded way. On the other hand, in trying to enjoy or appreciate a symphony there is not much I can *do* (in the *poiesis* rather than *praxis* sense): rather, I have to lay my mind open and respond to the music.

This is rather more a sliding scale than a distinction, but can we say anything about where sexual encounters come, or ought to come, into it? The idea of such an encounter is, presumably, to enjoy the sexual object as much as possible; this must mean that the more powerful, moving, or wholeheartedly delightful the encounter, the better. How far does this imply forcefulness? It seems certainly to imply some forcefulness or, rather, forcefulness at some points or in some aspects of the encounter. For sexual desire is desire for the object *per se* (not only in some one aspect) and implies that one wants not only to contemplate, or protect, or be tender toward it but also to *have all* of it—to merge with it and penetrate (or envelop) it, to make it respond, to put it in various positions, even perhaps, to make sure of possessing it completely (in a sense, to have power over it). It is hard to see how some or any of these particular objectives could be gained without forcefulness, just as other objectives could not be gained without taking time off from conquering to contemplate and respond, both in sex and in other activities.

2. Hostility. Hostility is hard to separate from forcefulness, because there

are reasons why any sort of *separation* from what is desired is apt to produce a feeling of hostility toward what separates. The ruthless businessman or football player sees his opponents merely as standing between him and his goal: he may feel neutral toward them, but he may easily regard them (as indeed they may be) as enemies. One may be in a hurry in a crowded street: normally one just sees the other walkers as (tiresome but not hateful) objects in the way, but in aggressive moods one may border on hating them, as if it were their fault. More importantly, one may feel that the desired object itself is hateful because the separation is *its* fault: "Where is that damned box of cigarettes?" This happens naturally with people: one may hate one's love object simply for not being there or available and, even more obviously, for deliberately not being available. In this way ambivalence is created, and nearly all (perhaps all) sexual encounters have some element of this.

Nevertheless, it seems that hostility is not a desirable element. Anger, or hatred, is justified or appropriate in certain circumstances; but getting angry with the innocent wife because she unconsciously reminds you of the cold and unsympathetic mother is like Aristotle's example of getting angry with the messenger who brings bad news: the target is mistaken. The feeling appropriate to what one sees as lovely or desirable is naturally love and desire, not hostility. One may set up, in sexual encounters as in other contexts, something like a competitive game: this is a kind of institutionalization of hostility (as well as of forcefulness) and may be either a useful form or a safety valve for aggressive feelings of various kinds. But this is different: the hostility is not overt but a form of play.

3. Power. Much more difficult is the part to be played by the exercise of power, whether in a sadistic or a masochistic role. Power can be distinguished from forcefulness and hostility, though the psychic connections are very close. If I make love forcefully or wholeheartedly, this is one thing; it is another thing if I display active hostility toward the love object, so that (for instance) I hit her or insult her; another thing again if I go in for, say, "bondage"—that is, I tie her up and display my power over her in various ways, and she does something similar to me. For I can engage in power activities quite coolly and, as at least it appears, without anger or hostility: I just want to make sure of, and enjoy, the power.

The question here turns on the degree of *security* that is reasonable for the person to demand and the forms that gaining that security will necessarily take. If there is anything to be said for power displays, it will not be the effect of the desirability of just being "on top." Both sexes, and all people, must in some sense desire power—not necessarily in a maniac de Sade or Hitlerian kind of way (as we might say, "for its own sake")—but in order to make sure of the desired object. It may well be—in fact, it clearly is—the case that different people and different sexes, naturally adopt different *means* to acquiring power: boys hit out, girls are slyly nasty, men beat their wives, women nag their husbands and so on. But this is a different matter.

Power has been given a bad name because of its abuses; but I am inclined to think that the suggested cure—to forswear it altogether—is worse than the disease. To speak first in general terms, it is plausible to say that aggression constitutes the most important practical problem for the modern world. It is, very palpably, *there in men*, and frequently comes out in destructive and disastrous forms. What we do with our sexuality, it might be said, can take care of itself but what we do with our aggression cannot, because it kills people. We (particularly if reinforced by some kind of "liberal" or tender-minded ideology) are frightened of aggression and tend to deny it; but this is no attempt at an answer. The interest of considering it in relation to sexuality is perhaps this: not only does it seem deeply woven into sexuality, but also the sexual arena seems to constitute a sort of model case—if we cannot handle our aggression in relation to our love objects, one might (naively) think, what chance do we have of handling it elsewhere?

It is thus simpleminded to try to abjure the need for power, but equally naive to suppose that notions like 'sexual pleasure' or 'love' will somehow in themselves abate or defuse it. On the contrary, the more desirable the object and the more totally and pervasively we desire it, the greater will be the need for power. It is important to see at this point that this need will naturally be both for power *over* it, in order to make sure of it, and for securing *its* power over oneself. Behind specific desire (even sexual desire) and its satisfaction lies a very basic notion, perhaps to be represented by such terms as 'feeling alive', 'feeling real', 'not just being half-there', or (to borrow a term from one philosopher)[1] feeling 'enmeshed' in the world. This has as much or more effect on happiness than the satisfaction of specific desires. We feel, somehow, that it is a good thing to *have* desires as well as to satisfy them (unless we are doctrinaire Buddhists—and that doctrine leads to something very like nonexistence). In order for this to be the case, there must be attractive objects, objects of desire, that (just because they are to be attractive) have power over us.

All of this is well known in practical living. The husband wants his wife to dress up in order to attract him (and, of course, eventually satisfy his desires). Someone who is in love or who (if that phrase is obscure) has the chance of seeing some object as sexually desirable in a deep and intense kind of way wants to preserve his image of it as powerful, as exercising power over him. He wants (sometimes, at least) to see the girl as a goddess, as overpoweringly beautiful, as irresistible. Men and women adopt various measures to achieve this, presenting those images of themselves that they think will keep the attraction alive or heighten or vary it. There is an element of masochism (to use a cheap word) in this, just as there is an element of sadism in its opposite—that is, in the desire to make sure of one's own power.

There seems no doubt—and this could hardly be otherwise and constitutes something like a conceptual truth—that this is powerfully reinforced (or perhaps instantiated as the model case) by the inevitable relationship of the young child to its parents. What makes it naive to suppose that adult sexual encounters consist of two free, equal, and "mature" people—so that we dismiss the whole idea of power, in any strong sense, as somehow disreputable or bordering on lunacy— is that the adults bring their past experiences with them. These experiences inevitably consist of feelings of total dependence (powerlessness) and feelings of extreme aggression and desire to control, since the parents (however loving) cannot help but but be sometimes absent, sometimes thwarting, and, therefore, sometimes creatures over whom the child wants to be able to exercise absolute power.

So far, then, we must conclude that though aggression in the sense of hostility is not conceptually involved in the notion of sexual desire and satisfaction, the ideas of forcefulness and power—both in the sadistic and in the masochistic sense—are necessarily involved. These are important conclusions, but we may also raise questions about how *much* power should be involved and how *often*— and the same for forcefulness. We can say that much will depend on the particular psychological states of the individuals concerned: different individuals need to "act out," in a sexual encounter, their various psychic needs at different strengths and for different lengths of time. This, given that people are as they are and cannot easily or quickly change, may be the most useful practical criterion. But we have the feeling, at least in extreme cases (de Sade or Masoch), that the situation is not ideal; we would feel this even if there was no question of other people's interests being at stake—if their sexual partners were totally compliant.

One part of this feeling may be the (extremely murky) idea that 'equality relationships' are somehow better than regimes in which one partner 'uses' the other: the thing ought to be "mutual," or they ought to do it "together" or "co-operatively." We are led here into problems discussed later (see Chapter 9); if we mean only that both parties (or however many parties there are) should *initially consent* to a regime, since both are people with equal right, well; but if we mean that the actual behavioral patterns, the nature of the (agreed) regime, should be in some sense 'equal' or 'mutual', then this seems much more disputable. This ambiguity runs through most of the words we tend to use in this context: it is in a *sense* "cooperation" if a sadist and a masochist get together, just as (conversely) in a sense two people who do not go in for power displays but conduct their affairs in an atmosphere of mutuality are 'using' each other.

Nor is it possible to wriggle out of the problem by suggesting that in power displays the other person is desired and "used" only in one role or part of himself—as a slave or as a tyrant, a victim or a torturer—whereas in "equality relationships" or relationships of 'mutuality', *more* aspects of the person are involved. This is just not true: a couple who kiss and caress each other at the same time with mutual pleasure delight in one role, or regime, whereas a couple who enslave and dominate each other delight in other roles—and why should they not?

We have to try to show that somehow there is more pleasure in mutuality or that mutuality is somehow more central to the idea of sexual pleasure, *without* meaning simply that mutuality is necessary at the first contractual stage (in making up the roles or consenting), which is not disputed but also not relevant here. What can perhaps be said is that the most immediate or direct response to what is lovely or desirable is simply to *enjoy* it: the idea of having to exercise power over you (to make sure you continue to see it as desirable) seems in a clear sense derivative. They are things, we might be tempted to claim, that might only occur—or occur in so important a way as to make sadism and masochism intelligible to someone who felt more insecure than he need be about his sex object remaining available and attractive.

In making some such claim, however, we should have to be careful to stick to the criterion of enjoyment rather than the notion of "mutuality" as some kind of ideal. It is commonly said that women entertain the idea of "mutuality" more strongly than men: they take less easily to the picture of men 'just doing things to' them or of themselves 'just doing things to' men. They feel that everything, or as much as possible, should happen *together*—that the two partners should be "close" all the time. This may connect with the fear of being 'used' and then abandoned. As Cressida says:

> Prithee, tarry:
> You men will never tarry.
> O foolish Cressid! I might have still held off,
> And then you would have tarried.[2]

This is, or might be, very much the same kind of insecurity about the love object as seems to be felt by the man who goes in for power displays: a fear of loneliness and isolation, an unwillingness to trust the mutual desire if it is not acted out all the time.

One might say that the most 'natural', direct, or immediate enjoyment was something like this: each partner is attracted by the body (person-inhabited) of the other; they get closer, interchange glances, touch each other, caress each other, and merge closely—the erotic tension is heightened during all this and eventually defused by orgasm. *Pro tanto*, there is no question of power displays nor really even of forcefulness (in the sense described earlier) because there are no *tasks*, nothing (in a sense) to do—it all just happens. However, there are severe limits on this picture not just for the conceptual reasons mentioned earlier (that is, that a really erotic object invites forcefulness for its thorough enjoyment in a harmless sense—exploitation and that power is needed to achieve security) but for the more general reasons that, like it or not, we are conscious creatures with wills, intentions, and purposes. The 'natural' or direct enjoyment described above is very like a purely animal enjoyment: the mind simply comes in as contemplating the *pathos*, the erotic pleasure that somehow just happens. Whatever may be thought of the virtues of contemplation as against action, the idea of action is deeply built into the human mind, and, in fact, the time limits of this "natural" enjoyment turn out to be fairly restricted. The two sexes may (or may not) differ, but both demand action: the woman perhaps says, "Let something now be done: caress me thus, make me feel thus," and the man,"I now want to do something: to caress you thus, make you feel thus."

All we can perhaps say, then, is something about flexibility and compulsiveness. If a man *cannot*, because of his overwhelming desires for power displays, enjoy at least something of the 'natural' merging, or if a woman cannot, because her fears about security (which may be very varied), release sufficient aggression to enjoy forcefulness and demonstrations of power at some time, something seems wrong. For, in the light of what we have said earlier, it seems that both of these are rightly, justly, and inevitably enjoyable. The admixture must depend on taste and temperament, mediated by negotiation.

NOTES

1. Robin Barrow, in *Plato, Utilitarianism and Education* (Boston, Mass.: Routledge & Kegan Paul, 1975).

2. *Troilus and Cressida*, act IV, sc. 2, lines 16-18.

5

INTEGRITY

'Integrity', a term much used by some modern philosophers (and in moral philosophy, something of a fighting word), is rather a mysterious piece of English. It has no formal opposite (as 'disintegrity' might be) and barely allows an adjective ('integritous' is sometimes used). It is, moreover, nearly always used in rather high-minded (not only philosophical) contexts: we might equally say either that its "normal usage" is to be found in those contexts or that it has no normal usage—it is not the sort of word that people commonly use over a cup of coffee or in doing business. We use 'trust' and its relatives ("distrust", "mistrust", "trustworthy", "untrustworthy", et cetera), and "honest", but not "integrity". One might almost think the word had been invented, or revived, or given a new twist in order to fill a rather special gap.

That is, as we may come to see, not *per se* discreditable; but it is a reason for caution. The man who has integrity, as the term is used, has some kind of virtue; the man who lacks it, some kind of vice. It is not immediately clear in what class of (in some sense, 'moral') virtues we are to place it. Is it a self-regarding or other-regarding virtue? Is it a virtue of the will, an executive virtue, like courage and determination? Or has it got something to do with the understanding of justice, like honesty and truthfulness? None of these seem anywhere near the mark. We have, then, to ask not only what integrity is but also what it is *for*: what *point* there is in it. We might then begin to see whether and how it can be applied to the sexual life.

Measure for Measure might be thought to offer some good examples. Angelo, perhaps, lacks integrity in a number of different ways. He purports to represent and enforce (as governor) sexual purity[1] but demands Isabella's body as the price for releasing her brother Claudio, whom he has condemned to execution on a (somewhat thin if we believe Claudio himself in act I, sc. 2, lines 134-44, 146-60) charge of immorality. When Isabella threatens to tell, Angelo says:

> Who will believe thee, Isabel?
> My unsoilid name, the austereness of my life,
> My vouch against you, and my place i' the state,
> Will so your accusation overweigh
> That you shall stifle in your own report.[2]

Thus, (1) he is perhaps untrue to the spirit of purity, condemning Claudio on a technicality; (2) he is certainly untrue to it in wanting Isabella; (3) he is in some way cheating by trying to force or blackmail Isabella; (4) he is willing to be untruthful in order to hide his sins.

The Duke (who pretends to go away but, in fact, disguises himself and watches what goes on to " see/If power change purpose, what our seems be")[3] is not normally accused of lacking integrity, presumably on the grounds that he acts with good intent or for good ends. It may also be relevant that he is the boss and is represented as having more or less absolute authority. Nevertheless, some at least of the *dramatis personae* might reasonably feel that there were certain ways in which they could not trust him after such a performance, however virtuously intended. since they have clearly been deceived. He does not, indeed, act as an *agent provocateur* (this might have made things much worse), but he was certainly pretending to be who he was not and spying on other people.

Isabella refuses Angelo's demands, even in the face of her brother's death. In talking to Claudio she says that if he agreed to the condition it "would bark your honour from that trunk you bear, and leave you naked": "thou art too noble to conserve a life/In base appliances." "Death is a fearful thing," says Claudio. "And shamed life a hateful," she replies, and earlier:

> O, were it but my life,
> I'd throw it down for your deliverance
> As frankly as a pin.[4]

With Isabella we feel inclined to say, not that she lacks integrity, but either that she has the wrong sort of integrity or that integrity is not a relevant virtue in such a situation.

I have extended these examples (there are plenty of others) because it seems important, with such an unusual term as 'integrity', to get the feel of at least some backgrounds where one might want to apply the concept. One point that emerges is some sort of rough distinction between two things. First, there is *honesty* (in the modern sense, not in that Shakespearean sense that, in fact, sometimes stands for the second thing as well)—that is, the virtue of someone who tells the truth, does not otherwise deceive, and does not cheat by concealment. Honesty is a subdivision of justice: being dishonest is doing wrong to others by fraud (rather than, say, force), as Aristotle puts it. Isabella does not do that; the Duke does it only if what he does is to count as doing wrong to others; and Angelo does it at least in (4) above—that is, in being willing to lie to gain his selfish ends. Second, there is something we may provisionally call 'honor', or 'being true to' something. Isabella is true to her own ideals and preserves her honor (maidenhood) even against stiff temptations (though actually it is not clear that she found them very tempting). The Duke seems neither honorable nor dishonorable; but Angelo may be thought not to be true to the ideal of purity in (1) and (2) above and, since he accepted his authority from the Duke, not to be true to his charge or duty as a ruler (3).

It is clear that there may be empirical connections between the two. Thus in (4), where Angelo is willing to lie, he is so willing *because* (in [1] and [2]) he is untrue to the ideal: he allows his selfish desires to override it, and then has to lie in order to cover up. This is common enough. But there can also be a conceptual connection. The really objectionable thing about Angelo (or one of the objectionable things) is that he creates the appearance of purity but does not act up to it:

> Lord Angelo is precise;
> Stands at a guard with envy; scarce confesses
> That his blood flows, or that his appetite
> Is more to bread than stone[5].

If Angelo had retained his honor or integrity, he *could* not have deceived nor lied nor been dishonest, at least in respect of this ideal. For part of the concept of "being true to" an ideal—any ideal—is that, in this respect, one practices what one preaches and acts and talks as one actually feels.

Does not the Duke disprove this? He deceives, yet does not seem to lack honor or integrity. No—for if the Duke can be construed as operating in the dimension of honor/dishonor at all, his honor presumably consists of the ideal of a just and conscientious ruler. This is his job and his duty, what he has to be true to. In order to do it properly, he has to deceive: but only in a way that, while it would be corrupting for other ideals (say, for certain kinds of personal relationships), nevertheless actually serves rather than corrupts this one. Or, if we want to say that it does corrupt it, we have to make out a case that such deceit does in fact detract from the good ruler. Similarly, a spy, at least in wartime, does not pursue a dishonorable profession, though he may have difficulty in preventing his professional demands from corrupting his other relationships.

For these reasons it seems best to say that the basic element in integrity is the idea of being *all of a piece* (as the root meaning—"wholeness," "intactness"— suggests or surviving nowadays only in mathematical uses, "integers" or "whole numbers"). The idea of honesty is built into this: if one is not all of a piece, then inevitably one presents different aspects at different times, which makes one un-reliable and—if this presentation is at all governed by blameworthy selfishness— also dishonest. Without blameworthy selfishness, a person might be governed by changes of mood, attitude, or belief. In an extreme case, he might be schizophre-nic but not dishonest—just unreliable. We do not talk of lack of integrity here, since *integrity* is the name of a moral virtue, where 'moral' at least includes some reference to the will or selfishness. Characteristically, as in Angelo's case, a man *shows* his lack of integrity by acting in some overtly dishonest manner.

Is this, then, a self-regarding or other-regarding virtue? Surely, both. There is a typical element of half-truth in Polonius:

> This above all: to thine own self be true,
> And it must follow, as the night the day
> Thou canst not then be false to any man.[6]

For the man who is true to himself, all of a piece, is at least *predictable*, even in the paradoxical case of the liar or dishonest man, *provided that he shows it* (and if he does not, one piece at least is out of place). "How could you believe me when I said I loved you, when you know I've been a liar all my life?" At least we know who we are dealing with, if not much else. But it is also a self-regarding vir-tue. We can have ideals that do not affect, or seriously affect, other people—im-ages of the self that we value, either as something to be strived toward or some-thing to be retained and kept coherent. We say, "I am importantly, or impor-tantly want to be, *this* sort of person." It is difficult to see how any human be-ing could not have a self-concept or self-esteem or an 'ego identity' of roughly this kind; we may even want to use words like 'dignity'. The image or picture is what *keeps him together* or makes him feel *worth* something (*dignus*). How could it not be good for him to be true to it?

We have, however, two options here. Is the basic sense of "integrity" such that I lack or lose it primarily when I am untrue to what I feel I importantly *am* or when I am untrue to what I feel I *ought* to be? Certainly it seems to be a mat-ter of being rather than doing, or being first and doing second. I may firmly be-lieve that I ought not to smoke, but if I fall victim to temptation, I do not feel at all inclinded to say I lack *integrity*—"will power" or "determination" would be in place, but "integrity" only in place (except perhaps in a very thin sense) if I have a strong picture of myself as *being* a nonsmoker (a dedicated athlete might be a reasonable example). Very well, now suppose Angelo had a strong ideal that he *ought* to be chaste but constantly fell victim to temptation. He is untrue to what he thinks he ought to be, but I think it is again only in a thin sense that we should say he lacks integrity: he is just a weak-willed sinner like the rest of us (and like some of the other, more 'human', characters in the play). The point about Angelo, as we noticed, is that he thought he *was* chaste, but he was untrue to himself. Integrity, then, has primarily to do with what a man importantly thinks he *is*. At the same time he has to value what he is in this respect: he must think it a good thing to be. So the answer is, in a way, both: it is his "better self" that he is true to, but the better self must also be the real self.

What sort of virtue is this? If we are right about its basic element (keeping oneself all of a piece or intact), it seems—though this sounds odd, because it is insufficiently high-minded—to be a kind of *prudence*. The good of integrity seems like the good of security, or invulnerability: the man wants to keep himself safe from disruption. At the same time it involves the ability to fight off temptation and, hence (sometimes at least), courage. Imagine a Christian in the persecutions: he has only to say, "All right, I'll make a token act of worship to the Emperor," and he is safe physically. But his self-image requires that he does not do this: he is, *pro tanto* (since clearly he is imprudent with respect to other goods, such as survival), prudent, for he thereby "keeps his soul in one piece" and he requires the courage to do this in the face of danger. Courage is relevant to a great many virtues or, rather, to their exercise: the essence of integrity is prudential. We have to keep the mind or soul safe as well as the body.

How important a virtue is this—how *much* of a virtue? Dante put the trimmers outside of the circles of the Inferno, although they were still severely punished, perhaps because he was not sure what they had done wrong; they *che visser senza infamia e senza lodo.*[7] In a way it seems to be an essential background for other virtues, as much as a virtue in itself: "infamy and praise" can only operate if one has *some* fairly constant picture of the self to which one must be true. Otherwise, one acts simply *ad hoc* ("These are my moral principles, but if you do not like them, I have others"). In the extreme case one would hardly be a rational creature at all. So in *this* sort of way, clearly, it is a very important virtue.

At the same time it seems to easy. All one has to do (it might be claimed) is to pick out and "identify with" those parts of oneself that are not likely to cause much trouble temptation or those that have a certain compulsive quality about them and, hence, will be easy both to identify with and act out in one's behavior. Did Don Giovanni—to move now into the more specifically sexual area—have integrity? We tend to say 'no' to this, but this seems to be only because he deceived women, not because he slept with so many. Deceit, as we have seen, implies a "bit missing." Suppose he had worn a placard saying words to the effect of: "I am a professional seducer; this will involve some lies (for purposes of seduction), so be warned (or encouraged, if you are the sort of girl who likes that sort of thing). Also I work hard at being true to myself in this respect—1,003 girls in Spain, and I feel I have not lived up to my ideals yet in other countries, but I am working at it"—now, what should we say?

I think we should say what most people would say about Isabella: that she did indeed have integrity but that the *content* of it was misconceived. For there is nothing in the concept of integrity itself that has any reference to content. "Honor," in just the same way, may consist of various things: there are honorable pacifists and honorable duelists. Integrity is not a "utilitarian" virtue in the sense that the person with integrity just decides what is in the general interest and then does it—it does not move in that dimension. Very often people with integrity do not decide at all: they just act, or act out, in a way true to themselves. It is tolerably clear that Isabella never entertained serious *doubts* about whether it was *right* to sleep with Angelo to free her brother; or, if so, they would not have been the 'utilitarian' doubts about where the balance of interest lay. They would have been of the form: "Can I do this thing and still be true to myself—can I live with myself and do it?" When Claudio says:

> Sweet sister, let me live:
> What sin you do to save a brother's life,
> Nature dispenses with the deed so far
> That it becomes a virtue.

Isabella replies:

> O you beast!
> O faithless coward! O dishonest wretch!
> Wilt thou be made a man out of my vice?
> Is't not a kind of incest, to take life
> From thine own sister's shame?[8]

Claudio, more utilitarian, sees the matter in terms of interest; Isabella, in terms of something like taboos ("incest"), things-in-themselves that must just not be done.

Such self-images and kinds (or contents) of integrity are very much to the fore in sexual matters: a person naturally says or thinks something like, "*For me*, sex has got to be. . . ." (licensed by marriage or at least love, a new adventure, aggressive, tender, or whatever). As the example of incest shows, many of these images are acquired by young and are virtually impossible to dislodge; and integrity, this kind of prudence, is essential if a person is to engage in sexual activity pleasurably or (often) at all. There are, at least in the extreme cases, certain things involved in sex that a person *cannot* do: of course, there is a (deep) sense in which it is his own wants, fears, and desires that set the stage, so that he may not wholly escape blame. It is not that he is under physical duress, but many of these lie so deeply that there may be little or nothing that he can, in the short term, do about it, and in some cases the body may simply not obey the will (as when males are impotent). So we have at least to *recognize* what our sexual integrity in fact consists of.

We must ask, however, whether there may not have to be some common content to *anyone's sexual* integrity—something that, if lacking, might make us say that his sexual activity and experience are *corrupted*. This is certainly to say something different about it than criticisms to the effect that it is 'perverted' or 'inadequate' ('impoverished'). It is to say, roughly, that the wrong kind of t thought, or desire, or practice has entered into the activity and spoiled it. Someone who is sexually corrupted, or who lacks sexual integrity, is not 'true to' what sex involves in a special kind of way. A perverse translation, for example, is a translation that is in some deliberate way wrongheaded or distorted. A corrupt translation is something quite different—the translator perhaps allows his journalistic instincts to take over and uses phrases that do not represent the original: he is not *faithful* ('true to') the original. An inadequate translation, something that merely fails to do full justice to the text, is something different again.

What is there in sexuality that we have to be true to? We gain some inklings of this if we reflect on why (apart from 'moralistic' reasons) we dislike the idea of prostitution, or the idea of making love to (or being made love to by) a machine, or even perhaps the idea of *asking* our sexual partners to *do* certain things to us in order that we may have certain sensations (as one might ask someone to scratch one's back: "A little higher, please, and to the left"). What seems to be wrong is that sexual or erotic desire—at least as usually defined—is not a desire for certain sensations nor even a desire for pleasure, or at least certainly not just these. The desire is for an *object*: characteristically, if not necessarily, for a person. We do not just want certain sensations *from* the object: we want the object as a whole to respond to our desire—this is what it means to desire an object rather than just to use it as a way of getting certain sensations.

A man could have a sexual desire for machines or for prostitutes: then he would desire them *as* machines or *as* prostitutes and would welcome their natural responses as such, provided that they met his original desire. This is different from, for instance, just wishing for an orgasm or a penetration or a bit of stroking; if *this* was what he wanted, then of course *anything* that gave him it would do. We hesitate to ask our lovers to do X or Y to us, because (though we may like the sensation of X or Y) we no longer treat our partners as sexual objects but rather as sexual machines. If it turns out that they actually want to do X and Y, then this is all right. Naturally, asking them might be a way of overcoming their shyness. But then we should be asking them whether *they wanted* to do X and Y rather than just asking them to do X and Y to us in order to elicit certain sensations.

Sexual activity and desire are easily corrupted, because certain pleasurable sensations are very strong. It does not follow, from anything I have said, that it is (in any direct action-guiding sense) *wrong* to ask and receive such sensations from one's partner or to seek them from prostitutes or machines or anything else. In this respect "corrupted" is perhaps a dangerous word. But insofar as we do this, the activity ceases to be "purely" sexual: it turns into a kind of appetite for raw sensation. In genuine sexual activity or encounters, a person wants the object to respond out of its own nature. He may try to elicit a certain response, but only if he thinks that such a response is "in" the object: for instance, a man may think that the woman would like to yield in a more dramatic and passionate way but is holding back (either through shyness or because she is not completely willing to be a sexual object for him).

It is quite difficult to participate in a sexual experience solely for sensual stimulation: nearly always we seem to want to give the sensations some kind of background, however cloudy. We want at least *a man* or *a woman* to do X or Y to us, and often this goes along with the idea of taking a certain role or doing it in a certain mode or with a certain attitude (dominant or dependent, for instance). There is here, of course, another possibility of corruption: this time we do indeed want a certain object (not just sensations), but the object is not in fact the one we are dealing with. This, however, is a different matter, and though it could count as corruption of a sexual encounter *with so-and-so*, it does not count as a specifically *sexual* corruption—that is, an interior spoiling of sexual experience itself. Yet, in practice it is often the chief difficulty. We cling, it seems, to wanting certain practices (X and Y) not so much because they provide us with sensations of pure pleasure (if that is what we want, we had better get hold of a machine) but rather because they seem to symbolize for us certain genuine sexual encounters that we confusedly seek—these are the *kind* of 'things done' that our ideal sexual encounter would naturally produce (and if that is the case, we do better to get clearer about what we really want and why and, perhaps, to change our sexual partner).

None of this should imply that there is, in any simpleminded sense, a "natural" set of sexual responses in terms of which sexual integrity could be ("naturalistically") defined. The only criterion is that they should be responses (of an erotic kind—otherwise we should not be talking of sex at all) *of the object.* Indeed, one might want to define 'response' in that sort of way. Human beings are very complicated sexual objects, with desires and techniques of their own. We cannot disqualify the use of sexual machines, for example, as 'unnatural' or "artificial" *in the hands of* sexual objects who actually want to use them on their subjects. For then these would be, as it were, extensions of themselves that they use for a genuine response—as if one happened to have an extra hand or some other useful piece of physical equipment. Sexual integrity consists of keeping the desire and the activity essentially sexual—that is, in brief, object-related.

NOTES

1. *Measure for Measure,* act III, sc. 1, lines 17-31.
2. Ibid., act II, sc. 4, lines 55-58.
3. Ibid., act I, sc. 3, lines 53-54.
4. Ibid., act III, sc. 1, lines 72-73, 88-89, 104-6, 117.
5. Ibid., act I, sc. 3, lines 50-52.
6. *Hamlet*, act I, sc. 3, lines 78-80.
7. *Inferno*, II, 36.
8. *Measure for Measure*, act III, sc. 1, lines 34-36, 37-40.

6

OBSCENITY AND CENSORSHIP

I want here only to try to get a bit clearer about two major questions. We may ask what the concept of obscenity is and what things empirically instantiate it (what 'obscene' means and what things are obscene). We may then ask under what circumstances, if any, people ought to be prevented from displaying or seeing—if those are the right verbs—obscene things. This seems the natural order of the questions.

'Obscene' does not just mean 'disgusting', 'horrifying', or shocking. People sometimes talk about violence or profit making as "obscene": but these are attempts to profit from the strength of the term, rather as some people call pay offers "derisory." I find certain foodstuffs disgusting but not horrifying or shocking. 'Shocking' is a pretty general term, perhaps not worth our while analyzing here: charging elephants are not shocking but can give me a shock (roughly, an unpleasant surprise). Obscene things may perhaps be a subclass of shocking things, when they appear. The important fact is, however, that the word retains sufficient of its original connection with *scaena* ("scene," "stage setting") to refer primarily to what is *visible*.* Obscene smells and noises are so by deri-

---

*I include this for the benefit of readers who share (as I do) the view that words in their normal meanings are very likely to retain some element of their root meanings.

vation—so, too, obscene words. Religious swearwords are not *obscene* words; sexual swearwords are, because they conjure up (or might if we were not inured) certain pictures. There is some laxity here: we talk, at least in the police courts, of obscene suggestions and obscene acts, though we are more likely to use the term 'indecent'. But, as this term suggests, it is not that we think the actual *acts* indecent in themselves—we have no objection to married couples performing them in the privacy of their homes. The suggestion, act, et cetera would not be counted as obscene unless it were in some way *inappropriately public*. A suggestion made to my wife would not be obscene, but the same suggestion made to someone I had met for the first time at a party might be.

It is an interesting question, not to be fully discussed here, whether there are other candidates for obscenity besides sex. What makes the question difficult is that, at least among most English speakers, sex is nearly always taken as virtually the only candidate; when it is applied to other things we are never quite sure whether it might not be a metaphor or an extended usage. We talk sometimes of people being obscenely fat, meaning (I suppose) that if they are as fat as that they really ought not to be seen. There are certainly some good candidates for things that ought not to be seen: for instance, torture or disembowelment or various (nonsexual) things that went on in Nazi concentration camps. I think it would be in linguistic order to suggest that such things are obscene, the concept not being totally tied to sexuality and perhaps not even totally tied to the body (though it is curiously difficult, actually, to get away from the body—no doubt because of the connection with what is visible). But I confine myself here to sexual obscenity.

For reasons already given (see Chapter 1), the view that sexual obscenity is simply a nonstarter (because sex is an appetite like any other and the sexual organs just ordinary parts of the body) is too simpleminded. There are reasons why we cannot but regard sexual organs and sexual acts as 'special'. This is evidenced—though this is not any kind of philosophical or justificatory argument—by the fact that everyone, or almost everyone, "makes a fuss" about *some* such organs and acts and has *some* concept of privacy with a sexual content. It is perhaps equally simpleminded to suggest that the matter can rest there. One may certainly make some kind of fuss and feel some kind of dislike if privacy is invaded, but *what* kind? Many housewives characteristically have the idea that neighbors ought not to see the kind of untidy messes that exist in a normal household, and so they clear them away before the neighbors come—this, too, seems to suggest a certain notion of privacy (what is private to the family), but the messes are not obscene even if visible to neighbors. So, too, I might pick my nose or scratch my armpits in private and dislike seeing others do it, yet not see it as obscene.

We might now be inclined to say simply that these cases are not strong enough and that obscenity requires only that it is very *important* that something should not be visible. This does not seem to work: it might be very important, in the army, that the dirt on my rifle or under my bed should not be visible to the inspecting officer (otherwise dire punishments befall me), but there is not the least temptation to use "obscene". It appears that it has to do rather with the *kind* of importance that is attached to something's not being visible, and the mystery is that 'obscene' seems most at home where we are most unclear about this. In the army case it is (partly) because we can see very clearly *why* I must hide the dirt that it does not count as obscene: I am pursuing a clearly utilitarian end. On the other hand, if we try to pursue the suggestion that it is just somehow, in some quite nonutilitarian way, "wrong," 'not fitting,' "indecent," or whatever, the trouble is that these phrases seem to suggest no reason at all. It is understandable that some people dismiss the whole idea of sexual obscenity as mere rubbish.

Nevertheless, this suggestion seems on the right lines—this is indeed, at any rate, how we *do* actually feel about sexual obscenity. Some light may be shed if we consider further why sex is 'special'. It is important here to get away from the idea that it is certain *things* or physical occurences *per se* that are 'special'— an idea apt to distract us in the context of obscenity because of its connection with what is visible. When doctors or nurses, for instance, deal with patients' sexual organs, there is no question of obscenity: at most there may be a feeling of embarrassment. The situation is quite unlike one in which a committee of the town council views a pornographic film (to determine whether it is obscene). Though both are no doubt equally virtuous, the doctors and nurses simply have no interest in sexual pleasure, whereas (derivatively) the committee has such an interest. What makes things obscene are not the things themselves (or not directly) but their connection with sexuality itself—by that I refer primarily to what sexuality *reveals* about a person.

Suppose, what is fortunately not yet wholly true in our society, that sexual encounters (and other sexual experiences, such as masturbation) were characteristically regarded as trivial—that is, people went through these experiences without their passions becoming seriously involved, perhaps reading books as they made love or with their minds only half on the job. Then I doubt whether, apart from prejudice, we should regard this (when made publicly visible) as obscene; or if we did, in nothing like so strong a way. It is the fact that, at least sometimes, people act out their deepest (or at least their strongest) feelings in sexual encounters that make them candidates for obscenity. We see them as, in a certain sense, defenseless against the outside world and against our viewing, emotionally naked.

This is a necessary fact about sex and not just a contingent one. It could be the case—though, for deep psychological reasons, it is on the borderline—that matters to do with excretion (commonly called "obscene") become commonplace, something to which people attach no strong feelings. This is true in some circles, although it takes a lot of habituation. It could not be true of sexual pleasure, not because it is a very intense *bodily* pleasure—eating and drinking can give rise to just as much intensity but have no touch of obscenity about them—but because it is a kind of desire for the body that goes to the roots of the human psyche and pervades all or most of it, which is why it is odd to think of someone reading a book at the same time. The person is *inwardly shaken* in a sexual experience. If someone suggested that we could "grow out of" minding whether people saw us in such states, I should like to hear him propose a training program that did not also makes us "grow out of" the intensity and vulnerability involved in the experience itself.

The case of the *voyeur*, which may seem opposed to this idea, is in fact parasitic upon it. Why should it be particularly exciting to watch the sexual act unless there was some element of the forbidden or at least the thrilling, in the watching itself? If everybody copulated publicly all over the place and one was raised in such a society, one could hardly be a *voyeur*, watching perhaps merely out of ordinary interest, as children are interested in the sex lives of animals. It would not be itself an erotic experience. So, too, with Candaules-type cases[1] —if somebody gets erotic enjoyment from *being* watched or from some other kind of visibility normally thought improper, it is that impropriety that is a constituent of the pleasure.

We have a kind of mutual pact to defend ourselves from emotional nakedness of this kind. I do not deny that a great part of what we have in mind when we call things 'obscene' (not the concept, but the general "idea" or the concept's connotations for us in our soceity) may be compounded by prejudice and other kinds of unreason, in at least two ways. First, as already suggested, we are too apt to tie the concept in with sexuality alone: there are, after all, cases of emotional nakedness, or various kinds of awfulness (torture), to which it could reasonably be applied (we do sometimes feel it "indecent" to watch the emotionally naked). Second, we are too apt to refer it simply to physical objects: of course, there is a connection between the sex organs and sexuality, but the connection is ultimately only contingent. It sounds a little cheap to say this, because the connection is so close, but when we are thinking about what is really obscene, it has to be borne in mind.

If this sheds some (admittedly faint and diffused) light on what obscenity is and on some of the reasons we have for attaching it to sexuality, we have yet to consider deeply enough what a *reasonable* attitude to the whole business might be. Part of the answer might be in the form of some moral theory or theory of practical action—for instance, R.M. Hare's idea of universal prescription. Thus, if we were considering what we ought actually to *do*, at a particular point in time, it might be helpful to say (this is not intended even as a caricature of Hare's views, but just to make the point) something like "Well, having the desires we do in fact have, how would you like it if *your* sexual privacy were so invaded?" (or whatever). But this does not go far enough, for we want to know whether we ought to have these kinds of desires. Nor, on the other hand, is it sufficient to say just that we are *bound* (because of the part sexuality plays in human life) to have them: we are certainly bound to see sex as 'special', but that still gives us a lot of latitude.

We might regard a great number of things as "special". To move along what seems to be some kind of dimension, we can use a special dinner service or set of glasses when the neighbors come or for "special occasions"; we can see our flag or national anthem as possessing some peculiar importance; we can have a special reverence for some great leader (Winston Churchill, perhaps) or for the reigning monarch; and we can see God and things connected with God—his name or temple, the "Holy of Holies", or whatever—as intensely 'special'. Notions marked by 'reverence' and 'sacredness' come toward the end of this scale. Now, if someone wants to put up a candidate for specialness, we need not only some account of why it is special, or what is special about it, but also just *how* special or important it is and whether the kind of specialness or importance precludes *other* attitudes being taken toward it. Thus, granted certain contexts, it would not be too hard to sketch out why the Queen, for example, should be regarded in a special light; but this leaves open the questions of how important (in this general sense) the Queen is—do we describe her as worthy of respect, or reverence, or awe, or what?—and whether we might *also* reasonably see her as, say, somebody to make jokes and satirical plays about.

These two questions seem often in practice to be connected. If we think that something is *enormously* important in a certain way, we naturally stress the appropriate way to view this thing at the expense, perhaps, of other ways of viewing it. It is difficult or impossible for Judeo-Christian believers to make jokes about God, though early Greek believers (notoriously Homer, assuming Homer to have believed anything) made jokes about their gods, at least until people such as Aeschylus and Plato made them pull their socks up. Judeo-Christians would say, probably, that this just means that the early Greeks did not take their gods very seriously. Similarly, if you can laugh at satirical sketches about the Queen, you cannot also give her the respect she deserves. Or, someone slipping on a banana skin (or whatever) and falling down cannot be funny, because the person might get hurt.

This is, in fact, a very curious idea. Of course, perhaps particularly for educational purposes, we might want *first* or primarily to stress what seems to be the most important *species* or description under which the thing can be viewed: I need first to get my children to see elephants as dangerous and only secondarily to show them that they are also lovable, amusing, and so forth. It is hard to see what would be meant by saying that only *one* description was appropriate. We might think that, if someone laughed at the man slipping and falling this indicated that he did not or could not also see it as a situation demanding help and sympathy, but this does not have to be so nor in practice is it always so. It depends—a point that is crucial for all discussions of censorship, pornography, and purity in general—very much on the sophistication and sanity of the observer.

We might ask, then, How important is sexuality? and Does it admit *other* descriptions? To the first question no short answer is possible: it must necessarily have *some* "specialness." But there does not seem any reason to suppose that a man might not, for instance, regard doing philosophy as equally (though in a quite different way) 'special' and be equally offended at examples of slack, trivial, or 'corrupted' ('impure') philosophizing. He might even object to philosopers being satirized, though Socrates seems to have been right in standing up during Aristophanes' *Clouds* so that the audience could see the original object of the satire rather than make a protest. The fact that sexuality has a *common* sort of importance, that it is important to all persons just because they are persons and have bodies and feel pleasure, does not give sexuality a *greater* importance. If one were to argue for the profundity of its importance, one would rely rather on some (perhaps semi-Freudain) view about the way in which sexual or erotic pleasure somehow *turned into* other kinds of desires and human goals. A true-blue Freudian might go so far as to say that sex was sacred, on the grounds that it was the prime source of human striving (the Life Force, or whatever). There are various difficulties with this line or argument; suffice it to say that we value what the force turns into as much as the force itself. Love would be a better candidate.

Turning to the second question, even if sex were of the highest importance, deserving terms like 'sacred', it would still not follow that other ways of viewing it were not in order. Certainly so far as practical sexual encounters go, some aspects of them seem to be depressing, boring, funny, graceful, clumsy, interesting, pitiful, beautiful, and lots of other things. But this aside, we do not characteristically think that the best way of viewing things makes other ways of viewing them "wrong" in any direct, action-guiding sense of that word. For example, no doubt the best way of viewing a Beethoven symphony is with a proper understanding of all its intrinsic qualities—its richness, majesty, and so on—but if a child plays the theme, we do not regard this as corrupting. We may say, particularly about the pop song, that it is a "misuse" or "abuse" or that it is "inadequate" or "impoverished"; if we mean only that it is not up to the symphony's standard, what is meant by the description is understood, but nothing follows about the desirability of *preventing* it.

We need to prevent (censor) such things only where it can be shown that the things in themselves, or by flooding the market, prevent or distract people (perhaps particularly children) from seeing the importance and nature of the original, which was Plato's chief concern. The question can always be raised whether, in this case or that, it can in fact be shown. No one, I imagine, denies the force of example and imitation: if *all* sexual encounters were represented to children as trivial "one-night stands" this would certainly affect in some way the chances of the children coming to see that sex had another kind of importance. The trouble is that there are so many variables here: even in this case, one could easily imagine a person reacting against, rather than falling victim to, the presentation—"There must be something more to it than that: these presentations do no more than motivate me to seek out the 'something more.'"

Almost everything seems to depend on how the representation is *received*. If the staging of *King Lear*, in which Gloucester's eyes are horrifically put out, was received by most people not as a work of art, requiring a certain kind of sophistication in which the general context and purpose were taken into account, but as a natural representation suggesting that such things were perfectly ordinary or trivial occurrences, there would be a good case for censoring or at least bowdlerizing *King Lear*; or if the story of the Crucifixion was received as suggesting that it was entirely normal to torture people to death on crosses, we should have to censor that part of the Bible. In fact, we rely, rightly or wrongly, on the presumption that there is enough sophistication—in effect, that enough education has gone on—for most people not only not to get the wrong message but to profit by getting the right one.

The position is much the same as when we find some child reading a lot of what we might call "trashy" literature. What we want to know is, Will this eventually help to lead him toward better literature or will it 'fixate' him on a corrupt idea of literature, either permanently or at least in such a way as to delay his proper progress? Most experienced people would tend to make two points: first, that much more can be gained (by way of accelerating the child's progress) by getting him to enjoy better literature than by banning the poorer; and, second, that you have to place a good deal of trust in the child—not because children know their own interests best but because there is such a thing as working with or against the grain of a person at various stages of development. A person has to be "ready for" the appreciation of certain books.

For this reason the simple point that people may *enjoy* certain representations (sexual or other) is by no means irrelevant to the idea of purity. We want, if we are interested in purity, to get the person to make a marriage between his enjoyment, on the one hand, and the truly good, on the other—and both partners must flourish. It is of no use just enjoying the bad and equally of no use just knowing that some things are good and being, in some nonpleasurable way, in touch with those things rather than bad things. This is why it is always an inadequate argument to point out, as many authors do at some length, that various representations ('pornography', for instance) do not show things at their best or as they really are; just as it is inadequate to point out that people enjoy them. The important features, for their education or chances of grasping the good, lie in quite a different dimension: what the person *makes of* his enjoyment and its object. Often it is very difficult even to begin to describe this sort of thing, but one could imagine, in however simpleminded a way, somebody reacting to pornography by saying either, "Yes, I enjoy it, and I will settle for that. Something better? Well, maybe, but it seems beyond my reach; it is too depressing to try for it—anyway, pornographic kicks seem to be all that is around these days; no one has ever shown me what something better would look like" or "Yes, I enjoy it, but somehow it is not really what I want: certainly I do not want to give it up—as I am, it is the only thing that keeps my sexuality a-live—but I will try to find something better."

To return to where we began, the concept of obscenity certainly applies to sex, because sex is special. Any attempt to represent sexuality as entirely *ordinary*, in the way that eating and drinking are ordinary, is misconceived, just as attempts to represent other special things as ordinary are misconceived. We need to adjust sexual and other representations with an eye on getting our children and ourselves to see what sexuality is really like and what the most satisfactory forms of it are like: without such an eye we lose our grip on the whole concept of purity and corruptness. Equally, we have to avoid the temptations to monism that lurk in this concept—temptations to which, perhaps, philosophers are peculiarly prone.

NOTES

1. Candaules enjoyed other men watching his wife naked, as the Greek historian Herodotus reports.

PART II

FEMINISM AND
SEXUAL POLITICS

7

SEXUAL INSULTS

The topics in Part II are more politically charged or emotionally loaded. For this reason it may be best to begin with a fairly well-circumscribed issue. I shall consider the idea that certain words (phrases) are insulting (degrading, sexist, and so on), and the connected idea that it would somehow be better if certain linguistic changes were enforced (for example, a common gender-free pronoun to replace 'he' and 'she', 'chairperson' for 'chairman', abolition of words such as 'nigger' and 'Kraut' and so on). These examples are heterogeneous, nor have I clearly described the two ideas (this is the major part of the problem); but they are made much of by feminists and others,[1] and it is important to see what can sensibly be said here. I suppose one sensible thing that can be said in advance is that there will be prejudices on both sides: conservatives ('retentionists'?) are no doubt apt to be too complacent, and linguistic revolutionaries to suffer from excessive zeal and fury. But this is merely a feeble attempt to lower the philosophical temperature, rather as the conductor taps his baton to reduce the noise level.

One thing seems fairly clear at the start: the mere *existence* of words is not, in itself, insulting or degrading. We do not have to name-drop Austin's work on speech acts to appreciate that words *per se* do not insult or degrade: men (and by 'men' throughout I shall mean, in accordance with a perfectly normal usuage, 'people' insult *by* (with, through, in) words—they *use* the words *to* insult. There is very little we can say about words by themselves without taking into account their meaning or use: we can say that they are long or short, hard or easy to spell, Greek or Latin, and so forth, but that is about all.

A model case of an insult would be to call someone a coward or a toady, although not every case of calling someone this is an insult. A benevolent priest or parent might say, "Yes, it is true you are a coward, my son, but God forgives": he is not insulting but commenting. Gestures are often less ambiguous evidence of the intent behind the words: for instance, a slap across the face with a glove in public as a preliminary to a duel—though even there the slapper might just be being petulant or perhaps is swatting flies. ("No, sir, I do not bite my thumb at you, sir; but I / bite my thumb, sir.")[2] To take a personal case: a famous and beautiful philosopher, perhaps a little quick to interpret genuine admiration as servile obsequiousness, once asked me with an air of objectivity if I had ever given any attention to the concept of toadying. This was, I think, her way of saying, "You horrible toady!": an insult, not because of any verbal form but because of her intent to communicate to me her contempt, disgust, and scorn. A word by itself tells us nothing either way. It is possible for a woman to pour scorn on the male sex just by saying, in a certain context and with a certain tone of voice, facial expression, and so on, "Men!"; just as it is possible for feminist philosophers to mention and use words like 'prick', 'chick', 'screw', and so on, but not to use them as insults or terms of degradation.

How is it then that we do, after all, talk of "offensive language," "fighting words," "dirty words," "insulting words" ("He used insulting language, your honor")? Does this not show that there is, in fact, something "in the word itself"? One thing is true: you cannot insult somebody by just *any* words. The limits here are pretty elastic, chiefly because of the possibilities of irony: a woman might insult a hopelessly inefficient man by saying,"You marvelous paradigm of male efficiency, you!" But there are some limits: try the Wittgensteinian exercise of attempting to insult someone by saying, for instance, "You glass of water!" or "You cirrostratus cloud!" Even this is not impossible, given a certain specified background and context: one of a group of hard-liquor-drinking speakers, or speakers who like their clouds in a potent cumulonimbus shape, might insult thus. But then this (and not something else) would be the background, and for such people it would be impossible to use *other* words to convey insults ("You piece of paper!"). We might say that though in principle any words could be used (that is, one could always imagine or even create a background to make their use possible), in practice for any actual group of speakers there are limits. (I hope my examples will make plain what 'in principle' and 'in practice' mean here.)

Let us say, then, what seems obvious enough, that certain terms are characteristically used to insult—*coward, toady, cheapskate, whore, ape,* and so forth. *Why* are these terms used? Presumably, because there is a characteristic recognition by both parties (insulter and insulted) that it is a bad, contemptible, despicable thing to *be* a coward, toady, and the rest. If there were not that recognition, the insult would not come off. Another personal case: I once said to an administrator and university politician, in a discussion about the education of teachers, "But that's just a political question" (no doubt in a certain tone of voice: I admit to being allergic to politics). He very justly replied to the effect of: "Coming from you, John, I think that's meant to be diminishing if not insulting to my question: however, maintaining as I do that politics is a respectable and important activity, I am not insulted." Similarly, if someone says, "You Limey!"–meaning simply "Englishman"–I am neither insulted or praised, since I believe it is neither bad nor good to be English despite what the *speaker* thinks.

What about the reverse case, where the speaker does not intend an insult (because he thinks that the characteristics he ascribes to the hearer are either desirable or neutral) but the hearer receives it as such (because he thinks the opposite)? Suppose a man says to a woman something like, "Hello, chick/doll/beautiful": let us assume that he is praising the woman in a certain mode or *species boni* (for looking nice) and let us also assume that the woman sees this not as praise but as some kind of contempt or insult. What should we say here? One might say that she may *feel* insulted but that she has not *been* insulted. This would be true even in those cases where the term might, sometimes, or even characteristically, be used to insult: for what counts is the speaker's intention. For instance, in some groups of English speakers 'bugger' is often used to insult but not in others (as Dr. Johnson's dictionary under 'bugger'"a term of endearment used by sailors"). Whether there *is* an insult, whether successful insulting takes place, depends then on an intent and an acceptance of a certain kind, themselves dependent on mutual agreement about the badness or goodness (more strictly, 'insultingness') of certain attributes as encapsulated in certain words.

"But is not certain language offensive merely in itself, just in virtue of the way it is received?" There is a sense in which we can say "yes" to this, but we have to be careful. We brand certain words as 'obscene', 'offensive', and so on, simply by virtue of the fact that many or most people in a social group dislike them or regard them as taboo. It is more accurate to say something like "thought to be obscene" or "taken to be offensive." In other words, the facts are that people *are offended*, but this is a long way from saying that they *ought* to be offended. The distance between the two allows us to raise questions like, "Is it really offensive?": "Would it offend the reasonable man (Aristotle's *spoudaios anēr*)?" The reasonable man, presumably, would not take offense if none is intended (and would not be offended by words *per se*). He might regard some linguistic use as boring, evidence of stupidity, or a too-limited conceptual scheme, or all sorts of things, but not as offensive or insulting. It is silly to talk of a bad philosophy essay as "an insult to the examiners."

I now want to move away a little from the specific idea of 'insulting', partly because I suspect that many writers on the general topic do not really mean 'insulting' (or if they do, they are wrong). It is difficult to say what they mean exactly: 'degrading' is a term often used, but I am not at all clear about what this means. We might try a sighting shot and say that though the speaker's use of a term cannot (for reasons given above) count as an insult, it may suggest a view of the world that is, in certain respects or contexts, improper; and might it not be so improper, or improper in such a way, that it could fairly be taken (by certain parties) as insulting or at least offensive? Might we not have to go back on what we said above? For example, suppose a feudal aristocrat remonstrating with someone in a patronizing kind of way: "My dear man." Could this not fairly make the man feel patronized ('degraded'?) and evoke the reply, "I'm *not* 'your dear man'!"?

There is certainly something in this but it is important to remind ourselves again that the vice lies not in the words but (in this case) the attitude, which must in turn be distinguished from a specific intention. The man might not intend an insult (feudal aristocrats commonly thought it was a good thing for someone if he was "their man") but his attitude might nevertheless be objected to. The difficulty is, however, that if we take away the specific intention, we have (in default of other evidence) only the words left, and they cannot do the job by themselves. The feudal aristocrat example was convincing only because we had already given a certain background and attitude: the aristocrat was already typecast as 'feudal' and 'patronizing'. Shorn of this background, the mere *words* "*My dear man*" tell us little or nothing. This, basically (though I jump a few guns), is why programs of a merely sociological or political kind to change the language, rather than programs to change the attitudes and people who use the language, are misconceived.

We need to see something of the difficulty in inducing attitudes from mere words, and I will give some (heterogeneous) examples. 'Slavonic Studies', the title of a respectable field of scholarly enquiry, is not normally held an offensive term: yet, 'Slavonic' comes originally from the same root as 'slave', Slavs having often been used as slaves. If contemporary Slavs got hot under the collar about this, it would seem that they are overreacting. This is a case, perhaps like many others (I do not know the root meanings of 'English', 'American', 'French', and so on, but many may well be equally disreputable), where the passage of time has obliterated offense. 'Limey' (= lime-juice-drinking British sailor) is not *per se* offensive, since nobody believes that drinking lime juice is objectionable: any offense must lie in the background, also somewhat passè. 'Philistine' and 'barbarian', in ancient Greek (*barbaros*), are ambiguous: either an inhabitant of Philistia and a non-Greek speaker (making sounds like "bar, bar") or uncultured and uncouth. 'Dog' is ambiguous in a quite different way: "Sly dog! Sly dog!" says the admiring chorus in Gilbert and Sullivan's *Trial by Jury*, but, "Back, you dogs!" reduces mutinous sailors to the animal level. "Puella" in Latin (diminutive of '*puer*', as boy, and meaning literally "a little boy," hence [?!] "a girl") might at first sight suggest a jaundiced Weltanschauung; but does the average Fraulein reasonably object to being called a little Frau? 'Darling' (='dearling', 'little dear') is not normally taken as objectionable. This raises the interesting question, much more important perhaps than any other, of what it is reasonable to regard as an improper attitude. I should be inclined here to say, for instance, that if someone regarded being called, even viewed, as 'little' in *this* sort of way as objectionable, there would be something wrong with his judgment. Of course, there are objectionable ways:

> Get you gone, you dwarf;
> You minimus, of hindering know-grass made;
> You bead, you acorn![3]

Lysander's words did not commend themselves to Hermia, but we do not all, therefore, have to be 'bouncing Amazons' like Hippolyta.[4] Finally, I have not heard any feminists object to the word 'virtue', which originally meant something like 'the characteristic excellence of a *vir* or male person, in particular courage,' and is, hence (in their view), a double insult.

Can we change attitudes by changing words? I do not know what sociological theory (if indeed that phrase connotes anything intellectually reputable) would say about this, but in practice it seems to work the other way round. It is at least not evidence of greater fraternity or equality that in some communist countries the term 'comrade' is insisted upon, particularly when used in some such conjoint phrase as 'comrade general': the *general* counts more than the *comrade*. Nor does the use, once more prevalent than now, whereby Christians call each other 'brother' and 'sister' seem to show the existence of more brotherly and sisterly feeling; or, even it it did, it would not show that those feelings *resulted* from the enforced vocabularly. But the thesis is not entirely absurd: some parents at least believe that by making the growing child say 'Please' and 'thank you' they engender not only the concepts of asking favors and of gratitude but also right attitudes (*actual* gratitude). "Assume a virtue if you have it not" and the discipline of having to say "chairperson" rather than "chairman" might, in some degree, change a person's attitude. But there is certainly nothing philosophically (nor empirically) necessary about this: the case is, at best, unproved. For there is a clear sense in which attitudes are independent of particular words, though they may emerge in words and use words. It would be quite in order to argue that such linguistic enforcement would merely *mask* undesirable attitudes, as when some married partners say "Darling" to each other through their teeth, as a kind of alternative to throwing plates.

This suggests a more general point, which is that any linguistic revision that masked attitudes or obliterated distinctions that we now enjoy would, *pro tanto*, be misguided. The fact that our language now marks distinctions by words like 'he', 'she', 'Miss', 'Mrs.', 'black', 'white', and many others is surely something we approve of: it enables us to give and receive information we would not be able to give and receive if the distinctions, with their verbal markers, did not exist for us. There is a much better case for expanding "Mr." into "Mr. (Married)" and "Mr. (Unmarried)" than for collapsing "Miss" and "Mrs." into "Ms." I am tempted to say, unphilosophically, that someone who did not accept the general force of this point would either be mildly paranoid (that is, thought that divulging information about himself in some way made him vulnerable) or else under the sway of a childlike view of justice ("Why should I give information if they do not?"). It is surely a desirable characteristic of any language that it should be rich and mark distinctions. There is supposed to be a language in which the exact social status of the speaker and the degree of authority with which he is prepared to back his propositions are given by different moods of verbs; whatever one may think about social status or authority, this is useful. Some people, indeed, talk of the whole apparatus of language as in some basic way being corrupting: it 'labels' people, or 'stereotypes' them, or assigns them to categories; or perhaps it is seen as somehow a barrier between a man and his fellows, something that spoils and corrupts (reifies?) the natural impulses of the heart. However, as philosophers should know better than anyone, we are not human without language, or at least not consciously rational. Language does label and categorize, otherwise it would not be language. I mention this only to suggest some of the possible unconscious bewitchments from which we may suffer.

It is certainly arguable—but arguable for reasons of clarity and precision rather than for political or partisan reasons—that we need *additional* terms in this area. Much depends, however, on how sophisticated the language-user is. Anyone that thought, for instance, that when authors and speakers said 'he' that they did not, in all but a few obvious cases, also mean 'she' would not be very sophisticated; nor would anyone who did not appreciate that there was an English use of 'man' equivalent to the Latin *homo* (member of the human species) rather than to *vir* (male), as in 'mankind.'* (I do not know whether German feminists object to the term *Man*, meaning 'one,' like the French *on*. French feminists might, if sufficiently impassioned, demand that 50 percent of the uses of *on* should require feminine suffixes. I offer these cases not to mock feminism but simply to show that *ad absurdum* arguments have some force. Referring to God as "he" is an interesting case, relevant to what I was trying to say above: if someone were to demand that God be spoken of sometimes as female or described by some neutral pronoun, this would be because he wanted to change the essentially patriarchal style of the Christian religion. This might be a good thing to do, but to do it would be, in effect, to change a good deal of what now counts as the Christian religion. If and when people come to want to change it in this way, the language will come of itself (as it obviously would if

---

*It is worth noting that in Greece, where "male chauvinism" flourishes more than in many places, the terms are similarly distinguished: anthrōpos = mankind, and anēr = male.

they decided to worship mother-goddesses). Trying to *enforce* a change is jumping many psychological and social guns.

Finally, I would like to point briefly to a linguistic area in which feminists and others would do much better to concentrate. It requires not linguistic change but linguistic or philosophical education, the lack of which is mainly responsible not only for a jaundiced view of women but for most jaundiced views. This is the area where words have to do with the kinds of *differences* between men and women (assuming for the moment, what I shall try to show in another chapter, that there are some). For example, the word 'do' in English is frequently construed in a far too "active" or 'task-oriented', a way (perhaps because male kinds of 'doing' get highlighted in a male-dominated society): it is taken to refer to something like the Greek *poiesis* rather than *praxis*, to use Aristotle's distinction (though there are muddles about this even in Aristotle). With this interpretation things like fighting, building, orating, making money, and so on count as doing, but things like contemplating, cuddling, comforting, and simply being there do not. (Think how important some of the latter are for child rearing.) Compare such remarks as, "Do you work or just bring up children?" or "Put down that novel and find something to do."

My point about this is simply that these interpretations or constructions are, in fact, *not* built into the language: they result from our misperceptions of it, and they can be put right not by political ordinances but by teaching people to pay more attention to the meanings of words. It is an open and interesting question as to which kind of 'doing'—*poiesis* or *praxis*—has the more intrinsic worth, something I have discussed elsewhere.[5] This question could not be raised by someone who was not prepared to relinquish his interpretation in the light of the linguistic facts. 'Active' and 'passive' represent similar prejudices, though the linguistic position is much more obvious: why should it be *better* to be 'active' rather than 'passive', an initiator rather than a respondent? What should be *meant*, indeed, by saying that *praxis* was more important than *pathos*?

NOTES

1. For example, Lawrence and Baker, among others; see Robert Baker and Frederick Elliston, eds., *Philosophy and Sex* (Buffalo, N. Y.: Prometheus Books, 1975).
2. *Romeo and Juliet*, act I, sc. 1, lines 46-47.
3. *A Midsummer-Night's Dream*, act III, sc. 2, lines 29-30.
4. Ibid., act II, sc. 1, line 70.
5. John Wilson, *A Preface to the Philosophy of Education* (Boston, Mass.: Routledge & Kegan Paul, 1979).

8

SEX DIFFERENCES

A good deal written on the topic of sex differences is bewildered (I particularly recommend part of an article by Marilyn Frye, as containing most of the important mistakes[1]). It is worth saying in advance that there is nothing wrong with or anything regrettable about people being different: nobody really wants a world in which they are not. To some people, however, differences appear threatening: either because they are just differences, which makes life somewhat harder to handle (though more interesting), or because they are frightened that some differences may be seen as evidence of superiority. It is clearly true that a difference *can* always be seen in evaluative terms: not because people are lunatic enough to regard a mark of differentiation as showing that a certain group are, *sans phrase*, "superior" or "inferior"—though no doubt such people exist, if any sense can be made of what they say—but rather because there is or always could be some context to which a difference was evaluatively significant. Thus, if men are (generally) more muscular, this makes them superior when it comes to shifting rocks; if women are smaller, this makes them superior when it comes to getting out of narrow-mouthed caves. What is important is to establish what differences there are and what they are relevant to.

I might also add, if only because some people seem to have doctrinaire ideas about differences in general, that there seem to be some contexts in which we welcome differences and some in which we do not: or more precisely, some contexts in which we welcome *some* differences. We welcome unity and similarity for all players in the string section of an orchestra, but a difference between that section and the woodwinds. A philosophy seminar would be dull or

66

impossible if everyone made the same, or even the same sort of, contribution: at the same time we require some similarity here—a similarity of intent or purpose and of some level of philosophical understanding. It seems that in all cases in which human beings do things with each other (I avoid 'cooperate', because it also applies to competitive games and wars, though these could in a sense be said to require cooperation—that indeed is my point) we require some general similarity of purpose or rule following—both parties must *fight* if there is to be a war—but also a degree of diversity, if only of contribution, for the activity to be possible or at least not totally boring. There seems nothing *general* to be said, apart from something such as the above, "for" or "against" differences. It all depends on what we want to do. I shall return to this point at the end.

The major philosophical problem about sex differences is the systematic ambiguity of certain kinds of evidence. That there are physical differences between the sexes is not denied. Thereafter, at least at first sight, the game seems entirely open. For if a certain feature F is always preferred, and perhaps *thought* to be 'innate,' by a society in the process of child rearing, how in principle can we tell whether F is in fact 'innate' or 'the product of social conditioning'? Thus, suppose that F is something such as 'taking the sexual initiative' or 'holding political power' and suppose further (what is not quite true) that no societies encourage or even allow women to do these things: How are we to tell (1) whether F is simply not 'in' women and that all societies are vaguely aware of this, so that they reinforce or channel this 'innate' deficiency or (2) whether there are no innate differences, F being merely "a social product"? It is, in fact, very difficult to conceive of an *experimentum crucis* here—for instance, some think that boy and girl babies start to behave differently at a very early age (say, one year)—before 'social conditioning' has a chance to get at them. Does this not prove 'innate' difference? Not a bit of it, other people say: there are differences in the ways that people (themselves "socially conditioned") handle, cuddle, or look at, or speak to, or in other ways treat boy babies and girl babies, which might account for the differences.

A rather better experiment (which, to my knowledge, has not been properly attempted) might consist of either leaving the babies devoid of any human influence from birth—no doubt robots could be designed to feed them, change them, and so on—or ensuring that those humans who did have contact with them did not know whether they were boys or girls. The former sounds somewhat cruel, and the latter a bit difficult, though not impossible. However, a determined environmentalist still might say that the human attendants (in the latter case) made some sort of subconscious decision to treat all, or some, of the babies in accordance with sexual criteria. This would be hard to verify, and, although the experiment seems well worth doing, it would not tell us all that much. For many of the alleged differences between the sexes are such that opportunity to display those differences could, logically, only arise after a high degree of human intercourse—and, moreover, intercourse that took account of the child's sex. An F such as "taking the sexual initiative," for instance, could only be verified under conditions that included the subject knowing that he (she) was male (female): and this, it might be said, makes verification impossible, since that knowledge (in a given society) might itself determine F. Social conditioning theories are often unfalsifiable.

There is also another problem of verification, which I mention at this stage to show that there is no easy way out. Some hold that we have only to point to societies (usually in the Polynesian Islands) where women do, in fact, display F in order to prove that F is "in the nature of" women. But that will only work for *abilities* or *attainments*. Thus, if a woman can be found to play chess as well as the best male chess players, this would certainly demolish the proposition that no women can reach that standard of attainment; if enough women could be found, we could no longer generalize about women's abilities in this respect. But this tells us nothing about women's *attitude* or *motivation* in regard to chess-playing. It is mostly items of attitude and motivation that sensible believers in basic sex differences have wanted to rehearse. Thus, if few women hold political power, this may be because they do not want to; in turn, possibly, dependent not upon 'social conditioning' but upon what is 'in their nature'.

Conversely, one might come across a society (Amazons) where women hold all or most of such power—but this equally might be due to a certain sort of social pressure, which goes *against* their 'nature'. Nobody denies that social pressure plays a part: the dispute is whether that pressure goes against or along with ("reinforces") some basic feature of their 'nature'—or whether there are any such features to be distinguished from those of men.

It ought to strike us that there is something extremely simpleminded in this sharp distinction between 'innate' and 'social conditioning', no doubt ultimately due to some Pavlovian or Skinnerian fantasy about human beings. The position seems to be that the physical scientists, the geneticists, and the experts on the brain can point (as yet) to nothing that directly correlates with significant differences. Even if they could, there would be philosophical problems to be solved. (There is something funny, not to be explored here, about saying one inherits a tendency to do the *Times* crossword or run for president in a way that there is nothing funny about inheriting red hair or a tendency to tuberculosis: the difficulty being one of translation from one language, the language of genes and chromosomes and brain circuits, into the language of social action and performance.) So it appears to be anybody's guess. Since the evidence of 'social conditioning' is highly visible, this has been seized on with undue force.

There is, however, a whole swathe of evidence of quite a different kind. To associate it with the name of Freud is dangerous, because this might imply agreement with Freud's particular views on women, or with his particular stories (for instance, penis envy); I mention Freud only because he first, or most clearly, drew attention to this sort of evidence and encapsulated it in the remark "Anatomy is destiny." It needs first to be shown that there is *room* for this sort of evidence. This can be done, perhaps, by asking whether anyone really believes that the sort of body one has is likely to make *no* difference to one's attitudes, mental postures, and general outlook on life and whether it can fairly be put under the heading of 'social conditioning'. I do not think that anyone seriously believes either, but in case anyone thinks he does I will give some imaginary examples. Suppose I am born a humpbacked, immobile midget, or suppose I have tentacles, or suppose children were characteristically stronger than their parents—does anyone now think that this would make no difference to psychological attitude? It would and the difference would be logically independent of (though always able to be reinforced or diminished by) anything fairly to be called 'social conditioning', even in the widest sense whereby that phrase included parental handling. Equally, it would in an important sense be independent of genetics: certainly it is a physical *fact that* I am immobile, or very strong, or tentacular, or liable to break if something bumps into me, but the fact will cause me to adopt certain attitudes (for instance, fear of destroying things because I am so strong, or fear of being destroyed because I am fragile).

It is important to see that this is a conceptual or necessary point, not an empirical one, for what actual empirical attitudes are likely to be forced on, or at least made very attractive ('natural') to, the actual bearers of bodily differences is a much more difficult and detailed question. We are here in an area of enquiry where one is never quite sure whether to use conceptual or empirical arguments—whether it is a matter for philosophy or psychoanalysis. Most psychoanalysts believe in some story about infancy and early childhood that distinguishes between boys and girls—that is, the story is different for each. The (not purely Freudian) story about the different love objects is a clear example: according to this, boys and girls both love their mothers (since their mothers, or stand-ins for mothers, feed them at the breast), but, thereafter, the boys have only to transfer their affections to other (non-incest-laden) women, whereas it is characteristic for girls to transfer first to their fathers and then to other men. Even this is, in some aspects, a conceptually necessary story. I mean that, granted that all babies are first fed by and hence in some sense get attached to women, this will necessarily make *some* difference to the subsequent history of their love objects. Much of Freud—almost all that can clearly be shown to be true—consists of semiconceptual points of this kind: so, too, with other psychoanalysts. *They* rely for verification on a combination of what the patient says on the couch, what his dreams are, what may be observed in very young children, and what his involuntary symptoms and voluntary behavior are in everyday life, apart from the more indirect evidence of anthropology, religion, and the like. All this, as I have said elsewhere,[2] adds up to a perfectly respectable set of verifiable propositions, whatever may be thought of their individual truth and falsehood. But here I shall try to see what can be said on conceptual grounds, combined, perhaps, with a little common sense.

Such conceptual necessities as there are stem from the point made earlier: that a young creature's body is bound to affect his mental stance. This is not just because bodies and their interaction with the world are inevitably important to any creature but because the infant's world is one in which his own body and, by comparison, other creatures' bodies play a major part—in the absence, that is, of those mental or intellectual features that the infant only gradually comes to acquire. This is not to say that infants do not have desires and emotions; lacking certain controlling mechanisms, they have them in a more passionate and 'raw' form than adults or even than young children. The point is that the *targets* of those desires and emotions, the material that is likely to shape them and give them direction, will often be something bodily or physical. The difficulty is to determine what this implies for boys and girls.

It seems to imply at least this: that the boy's greater physical strength (in terms of output—I am not talking about endurance) and musculature, together with a certain speed and crispness of bodily movement (boys run faster than girls, throw balls harder, and so forth), are likely to influence his attitude in the direction of *agent* rather than *patient*, initiation rather than responder. The possession of a penis, which appears to him to *do* something, as against a vagina, which does not so appear, may reinforce this or be taken merely as symbolic of it. This difference remains with children, other things being equal, until puberty when it is strongly reinforced. Erections of the penis are more obvious and greater physical strength more apparent; conversely, the girl's center of gravity shifts downward— she becomes more obviously slower and physically weaker by comparison, softer, fatter, and so on: a different kind of object—and certainly a different kind of *erotic* object.

That this will make the two sexes vary in a dimension that it may not be too misleading to describe as 'aggression' seems wholly obvious. Boys come to see themselves more as acting on the world; girls as responding to it. These are both kinds of "doing," and by no means is the whole of the child's attitude straight-jacketed—boys will respond, and girls "aggress" (or whatever verb is suitable). But, in general, we sense the difference that is clear when, for instance, one watches either sex playing tennis. It is not that the girls are, in principle, less well muscled or strong or fleet of foot, yet they hit the ball much less hard and crisply and with less of the 'killer instinct'. It is not at this later age just a matter of physical difference but of engrained attitudes.

Even if this general picture is subject to alteration and adjustment, it remains true. We must remember that much of the adjustment may itself be due to psychological, rather than 'social' causes. The Freudian story of transferred love objects would be one possible example of such causes; another, just as obvious, would be the effect of identifying with the mother (who, however feminist and aggressive, will almost certainly appear to the young child as "the one that feeds" or "the one with the soft breasts"). The degree of alteration possible within these (anatomical and psychological) parameters must be limited. It is not absurd to talk of 'the female role' and 'the male role', so long as we are careful not to interpret 'role' too narrowly. We are talking, not of (other than physical) *ability* (a matter in which, insofar as we can disentangle it from motivation, there seems to be not much difference between the sexes) but about a general motivational stance.

A word of warning here. It is entirely possible, indeed predictable, that either sex may at some point wish to *deny* or rebel against these roles or stances. (Transvestism is an obvious example: the man is saying, "I wish I were a girl— if I dress thus I can, temporarily, be one or at least pretend.") This may happen for all sorts of reasons, most of which are likely to be unconscious. One good candidate is simple *envy* of the opposite sex; men are said to envy women's natural creative powers, and the *couvade* (when men imitate pregnant females) is quoted as a possible piece of evidence; the envy of women for men's roles is also clear. It is, then, by no means necessarily good evidence if a person makes this denial: a man may *say* "But I am not like that at all, I am naturally soft and pliable" or a woman may say, "I am as aggressive as anything, hard as nails," but it is more than possible that they are speaking in an attempt to convince themselves (and others). Contrary to a fantasy that we all like to indulge, an individual is *not*, or certainly not always, in the best position to know what he is really like and what his deepest feelings are: many of them are hidden from us and perhaps more apparent to others (not only our psychiatrists). People create and spend a lot of time and energy in sustaining images of themselves that they need (for some psychological reason or another): images that impinge on the area of sex differences are not immune from this—indeed, the more emotion-laden this area becomes, the more false images of the self are likely to be generated.

How far and in what sort of detail this general account would be verified by psychoanalytic enquiry is a matter beyond my scope: I have aimed here only to show that there must, logically, be *something* in it and to open the reader's mind to the possibility and respectability of that sort of enquiry. Pursuing the account's general implications, however, we can see at least some possibilities. First, it is likely that certain jobs (tasks, services) will, in general, fit or suit one sex rather than the other (again, for motivational reasons rather than for reasons of straight ability): those that require good observation of people, pliability, tenderness, patience, endurance, and other qualities that might form an expansion of the notion of 'passivity' or 'responsiveness' will suit women; the more 'active' or 'initiatory' qualities of men fit better into other jobs. This more or less fits the traditional picture, but this is hardly surprising, if that picture is based on some intuitive understanding of sex differences (rather than on pure myth). Second, since sex differences will very likely be emphasized in specifically sexual encounters, it is likely that the man will be the wooer or initiator, and the woman, the wooed or responsive. Characteristically, the women will see herself primarily (I do not say only) as a responsive object and will want to be beautiful;

the man is attractive in another mode and more connected with activity, strength, and some kind of performance. "Man proposes, woman disposes." This, too, is traditional though not invariant. Third, it is more likely that the woman will be concerned with the inner world of feeling, emotion, and personal transactions than will the man, who by contrast will 'project' himself more into the outer world of science and abstract thought (it is not, in my view, accidental or 'socially' determined that novel writing has been one of the few visible-product fields in which women have excelled—of course, they excel in things which a male-dominated society may not score highly, such as child rearing or tending the sick). Many women may find the mere possibility of visible achievement vaguely threatening, just as men find passivity threatening or alarming. "Women keep trying to bring personalities into everything, they never keep their categories clear, they're not interested in *selling the product*," a man said to me once. And a woman, "Men seem to think that 'reasonable' equals 'logical': they put things in watertight compartments, they're always trying to *make* something out of the world instead of enjoying it." Finally, as passive respondents rather than active initiators, women are more likely than men to want security and men more likely to want variety—this, too, has sexual implications that are traditional.

I do think it likely that some, at least, of these differences have a genetic background; it seems unlikely that they are *all* due to the kind of early infantile reaction that I have briefly described. Not that such reaction is insufficiently potent to account for such differences; but the chances are that the physical differences go along with brain differences, as they clearly go along with glandular and hormonal ones, which also affect the situation. Animal behavior may be thought to shed some light on this; it is hard to believe, to use old-fashioned language, that Nature did not back the reproductive and sexual roles of the two sexes by some kind of psychological differences having the same general force. However, if there is direct evidence for this, I am unaware of it.

I come back now to where we started: the existence of differences. Assuming that there are some, what should our attitude be toward them? I said earlier that, "It all depends on what we want to do." Clearly, much of the answer lies here. There are certain jobs, roles, tasks, or modes of being that are, for reasons quite unconnected with sexuality, desirable to see done well: sending rockets to the moon, comforting, fighting, healing, and so forth. For these we simply accept the differences and use them for the general good. But what about sexual encounters themselves? Do we want to move in a sort of unisex direction (insofar as we can influence ourselves) or in the direction of reinforcing (magnifying) the differences?

The arguments for reducing the differences are plain enough. If men and women are (comparatively) more like each other, there is less chance of either being straitjacketed into particular roles. The man need not always be on top, the woman can wear trousers, and the man can behave in a "feminine" way and the woman in a "masculine" one. Moreover, the diminution of the role strait-jacket might make it more possible to achieve better communication among the *people* concerned: each sex would no longer have to approach what might otherwise seem like a totally alien being but could deal with someone more like himself (herself). If the roles are too heavily reinforced, men and women come virtually to occupy different worlds, use different languages, and share less common concerns (rather as in classical Greece or most historical periods).

It might even be thought, in this light, that *love* (no doubt a desirable thing) is thereby made more possible; but this would seem to be a mistake, since love (like most human enterprises, as we said earlier) demands difference as well as similarity—otherwise it is a kind of narcissism, when one loves only a mirror image of oneself. In one of the most touching scenes of all literature, Hector says goodbye to his wife and child on the walls of Troy before going out to meet his death at Achilles' hands. Nobody can deny that this is a love scene, that Hector loves his wife, and even that he loves her "domestically" (she is not just a 'sex object'). Yet, he ends his remarks to her by saying:

> Go home, look after your own affairs,
> Your loom and distaff: order your servants
> To be about their business. War will be men's business,
> All men who were born in Troy, me most of all.[3]

The arguments in favor of highlighting the differences, or at least of not reducing them, need to be stressed (though in a sense actual *practice*, rather than what is too often written on the topic, stresses them already). The point is simply that sexual desire is the desire for the other's body. Now it is difficult (unless one is a narcissist, and the sex lives of narcissists are hardly satisfactory) to make much out of one's own body or similar bodies. In order for the pleasure to be intense the other's body must be *different*—up to the point of grotesqueness, the more different (alien, mysterious, attractive), the better, which the sexual point of romance (and of other kinds of romance, particularly the romance of travel: nobody wants to see the town next door). There is, in fact, something almost like an incest taboo on women (and perhaps men) who are too familiar, too similar to men, or too much "good sports" who mix with men in all contexts. Some primitive tribesmen insist on going to other islands to find their mates.

This is why both sexes characteristically go out of their way to highlight not just sexually desirable or erotic features but those features that are different from those of the opposite sex; this is also why women at least tend to generate a certain concept of privacy and mystery that incites the interest, not to say lust, of men. Putting it another way, there seem to be good or at least understandable reasons why a person out for a fully pleasurable sexual experience would want to heighten the *tension* between the two sexes—stressing differences being one obvious way of heightening the tension. A Tristan and Isolde or Lancelot and Guinevere scenario has "more to it" than a scenario with the girl next door, who might almost count as one's sister. There was even a time when women dreamed about Arab sheiks in the mysterious desert (Rudolf Valentino) or, more recently, about Greek fishermen.

One of the chief difficulties of sexual encounters lies here, and I simply mention it without any serious attempt to describe a cure. It is that while with some parts of ourselves we want similarities and cooperation to be stressed—we want to be able to trust the partner, to feel safe, not to be raped if a woman, not to be smothered in suffocating feminity or bored by the same old "good sport" if a man, and so forth—with other parts of ourselves we yearn for the different: the demon-lover or the *princesse lointaine*. How can the same partner satisfy both needs? It is, at the least, inconvenient if he (she) cannot. Perhaps some form of acting or role taking would provide a partial solution, although this seems phoney. More plausibly, it may be that we can learn to view people more flexibly: to see both their similarities and their differences, both their familiarity and their mystery, or both their trustworthiness and their distance from us. As this is far too generalized a suggestion, I leave it to others to improve on.

A great deal of unnecessary trouble is caused by the failure to grasp certain necessary truths in this area. Thus, the fantasy of having a "classless" society is embraced by many feminists as a kind of overall model for, or at least in parallel with, having an 'androgynous' one.[4] Now it would be, in principle, entirely possible to have "androgynes" rather than men and women, given sufficient biological and psychological techniques, but it is not possible to have a classless society. For, since there will always be *some* differences between people, they will fall into various categories or classes. Further, it is hard to see how some at least of these classes would not be, in some degree and for some purposes, evaluative: how we could not, for instance, avoid using such terms as 'pretty', 'ugly', 'intelligent', 'stupid', 'strong', and 'weak', so that certain classes (so described) would, *pro tanto* and for certain purposes, be valued more highly than others. What we can do, of course, is to try to say something about *what* categories and classes we should single out in this way: Marxists might think it right to abolish or at least diminish economic classes, but this must presumably mean that they think other classes based on other criteria would be preferable, since plainly some classifications will fill the vacuum. Similarly, feminists who disapprove of sex differences and who wish to abolish them must think other vacuum-filling differences to be preferable and must show how, by abolishing sex differences, these other preferred differences will be more popular.

A serious attempt on this problem would necessarily involve trying to answer two general questions. The first is, What categories and classes are—either by conceptual necessity or by deep and nonnegotiable empirical fact—*given*?

Thus suppose, speaking from a male (and no doubt "sexist") viewpoint, one was worried about the existence of really ugly women, because they seemed seriously and irremediably handicapped (of course similar arguments apply to men): then one might find oneself thinking that this is all the fault of males, who are using categories that ought not to be used. They should not see women as pretty or ugly. Yet, does anyone really believe that the whole business of judging appearances, either from the strictly aesthetic or the erotic point of view, is dispensable in this way? Could we imagine a society in which all such terms as 'pretty', 'dainty', 'dump', 'graceful', and so on, were not used at all? And even if we could, would we want it? Of course, one may say (and this has been said even by patriarchal Victorians) that less importance ought to be attached to this category as against others, that the soul or the mind ought to count for more than the body but that is a different matter. If one recognized that the pretty/ugly category was not expellable (how could appearance *not* matter quite a lot to people?), one might rather prefer to face these facts and achieve some kind of rough justice by compensatory measures—like the tribe reported by Herodotus, which awarded dowries to women in inverse proportion to their beauty.

It seems fairly clear that a good many categories are in this sense inexpellable, because they are based on standard human interests that derive, conceptually, from what it is to be a human being. For instance, some concept of property is not inexpellable, even if that concept is filled out only by such items as the use of one's own body or the right to retain a piece of property for use over a certain time period (for example, food while you are eating it). Granted also that different individuals will be more or less prudent and knowledgeable, it follows that some people will be better at managing and expanding their property than others: "rich" and "poor," in a general sense, are inalienable categories. So, too, with categories more potentially relevant to sex differences: the ability to put out force, to endure with patience, to make quick practical decisions without bothering to sympathize more than necessary, to sympathize sufficiently in order that those decisions be based on a genuine grasp of interests, or to be tough-minded and tender-minded—these and many others are not concepts (and, hence, not classes or categories) we can avoid having. One of the difficulties experienced by feminists and other movements with an essentially political concern (Marxists are a good example) is that this concern highlights for them categories and classes that are *socially* produced or propped up, so that it looks as if they can be abolished or diminished by social or political means. But there are many categories inevitable for any society, and even those categories that appear to be merely "social products" are usually only specific forms of more basic and inalienable categories: we can abolish the forms but not the categories that underlie them.

The second question, which could only be tackled after the first, is, What categories are *desirable*? There is something very odd about this question, because it is hard to see how a *category* could be desirable or undesirable in itself: it all depends on the purpose for which it is used. No one objects, in compiling telephone directories, to distinguishing people whose names begin with *W*; but if it were thought that people whose names begin with *W* should be shot, it is a different matter. What we complain about is *irrelevant reasoning*, not the category *per se*. We normally think that whenever anything is to be gained by constructing or using a category, then we ought to use it: we need as many distinctions as possible, or at least as many as are necessary to fulfill our (very varied and multifarious) purposes in human life.

However, we could suggest that certain categories were, under normal conditions, more relevant or of wider relevance to human interests than others. The distinction between people and nonpeople might be an example; conversely, we might say that, though being black was relevant to playing *Othello* or distri- buting suntan lotion, the relevance of this category did not extend much further than this (or should not, in a sane society)—that for more important human interests such as food, education, political power, and so forth, blackness was irrelevant. One difficulty is that our interests inevitably and rightly change, or change their form, when external conditions change, so that it is hard to specify some category as *always* of lesser importance. Even blackness might be very im- portant if, for instance, we lived under conditions where it was essential to be able to merge imperceptibly into a dark jungle to avoid being eaten by lions. The existence, or even the possibility, of external enemies (natural or personal) makes a big difference. We sometimes suffer from the illusion that we can make 'society' just what we like, thereby enabling ourselves to order our categories in accordance with some overall ideal.

How, in this light, do the differences and categories discussed by feminists come off? Well, it is true that the relevance of 'being a woman' or 'being a man' must depend on what we think to be nonnegotiable differences between the sexes, if any. Also, it is true that there will be, at least potentially, 'feminine' attributes available to men and 'masculine' ones available to women; it is naturally desirable that people should be able to perceive, use, and act on as many cate- gories as possible. This, feminists have insisted on rightly, if *ad nauseam*: it is, in my judgment, the only point that justifies anything to be called a women's *liberation* (or a men's liberation) movement at all.

What does *not* follow from this—what, in fact, is diametrically opposed to it—is the idea that particular roles, categories, and attributes should be masked or muted. For these enable various forms of life or kinds of interaction to occur that we think desirable: games that we like to play. Feminists show some con- fusion between the idea of a role or attribute that is impregnated with a superior or inferior political status and that role or attribute in its own right. Take for example the idea of being "on top." This might be interpreted politically to mean that the role of women was—even when they did not want to and when it had not been negotiated—just to do what they were told or to take orders. But if interpreted sexually—I mean, simply in bed—we should adopt a different attitude. We should say that the role of being 'on top' was a good thing to have, since it allowed a certain form of sexual interaction; and instead of wanting to abolish or mask it, we should say rather that everyone (women as well as men) should be allowed and encouraged to enjoy it (and to enjoy being "underneath")—not that people should only be allowed to lie side by side in bed for fear of the political implications. It is difficult to think of any roles, even those that might be thought politically suspect, that we should want to abolish in this way; taking and giving orders, winning and losing in games, and ruling and being ruled are all things that human beings need to experience and can enjoy. The *negotiation* of these roles must, of course, be such as to produce justice, a topic considered in Chapters 9 and 10.

I am saying, then, that a rational attitude (a "truly liberated" attitude) would involve not diminishing but extending the roles and attributes of both sexes—provided that it did satisfy human interests and that it did actually suit the natures of the sexes. It would be nice for men, insofar as it is in them (and certainly it is in many men), to show themselves as tender and protective in child rearing and other situations, as women are supposed to be; to welcome women taking the sexual initiative; and to accept their own passivity. But we should lose something if they could not also be, or continue to be, Lancelots or Tristans or Lawrence-like heroes or if they were not, sometimes, masterful and (in a broad summative sense) 'masculine'. Similarly, it is highly desirable, under the same conditions, that women should be able to be crisply analytical, competitive, tough-minded, and so forth; but a good deal would be lost if they could not also be Guineveres or Isoldes, melting and dewy-eyed creatures of grace and charm, roses (by any other name). As we saw in Chapter 8, none of our descriptions here need be insulting, unless we insist on making them so for political reasons. We may turn a proper and much-needed concept marked by "virility" into "machismo" or "chauvinism"; or one marked by 'feminine allure' into 'a dumb broad' or 'a hooker'. It is silly to do this, as we should mark and enjoy the categories we need. "You're as delightful as the dew and as refreshing as the rain: isn't it a pity that you're such a scatterbrain?" Well, it is a pity, but this is not a reason for not being delightful and refreshing.

Perhaps I may be allowed one final plea, following from or enlarging on this. There is such a thing as being passive, as being a sex object or as being viewed erotically by the eyes of the Sartrean "other." This is one (if only one, but at most one of only a few) of the most basic or general modes in which human beings exist. How basic and important this is appears in the fact that perhaps the worst or most deeply wounding attitude one can adopt toward another is represented by "You disgust me." Disgust is worse than dislike or disapproval, worse even than hate, for it implies a total turning away from the person, a complete rejection. It must, conversely, also be true that the best (or one of the best) 'pro attitudes' toward a person will be represented by "You are physically very attractive." This may not sound very high-minded: all of us would like, or at least like to believe that we would like, to be admired mainly for our nobility of soul, profound intellectual acumen, or moral virtue. Well, perhaps we ought, and it is (just) possible that we actually do; in view of the evidence above, however, it is likely to be at least partly self-deceptive to suppose that disgust and its opposite cut little ice with us.

I say 'physically attractive' because the word 'beautiful' (as noted in an earlier chapter) is a little too specific. But, speaking now as a man (male), where I feel on safer ground, it seems clear to me that anyone who believed that men view women in this mode only as pretty little things, dispensable packages of sweetness to be used and thrown aside, simply would not have begun to understand how men (when they are being honest with themselves) really think. Beauty is immensely *powerful*: this is evidenced by a wealth of literature and myth as well as by obvious conceptual arguments. It is also something that, if you have it or some of it, is very difficult to confront, precisely because of its power—combined, that is, with the fact that it is a *passive* power. If one is admired for some performance, one may blush; it is perhaps easy to shrug off, because the person is not admiring *you* so much as what you *do*. One is not simply an object being *looked at*. The feeling that often goes with beauty is one of great vulnerability: even if the other approves and admires, one is still just there at the other's mercy.

My guess would be that nearly all women (and, no doubt, men, too, when put on the spot) find this difficult to tolerate. Because of the difficulty, itself a function of the importance of beauty, there will inevitably be some kind of denial (the rejection of compliments about one's appearance as "irrelevant" or "insulting" would seem an example). Not many women even *think* of themselves as beautiful: they see themselves, perhaps, as pretty, or passable, or "having a nice figure" or "good bones," or they may even descend further into the particular and think about whether they are "looking their best," whether their hair is clean, or whether their clothes suit them. Even those who know that they are beautiful do not, commonly, feel it: Helen of Troy never mentioned nor appeared to believe in her fatal beauty, though she had plenty of evidence. This goes far deeper than the idea that it is somehow "immodest" or "boastful": there is a deep reluctance to admit the power of beauty, which is something that men (admittedly in a very confused and tiresome way) spend a good deal of their time feeling and trying to come to terms with, and which has very little to do with whether a woman has washed her hair recently or is wearing fashionable clothes.

Men are, of course, in their own way equally frightened of this (which is why they sometimes pretend to themselves that women are just there to be 'used'). But I want to stress the point that to take it seriously involves a good deal more than just accepting the word 'beautiful'—it involves connecting that concept with others that give one some idea of the power of beauty. Thus (for obvious reasons, connected with early childhood), whatever may be marked by 'mystery', 'allure', 'glamour', 'remoteness', and other such terms takes us back to some understanding of the roots of beauty: beauty is not something that is confined to the familiar, the well-known, the ordinarily lovable. In one aspect, perhaps, it recedes infinitely (we never quite catch up with the Form)—something we have to come to terms with. Any women who thought that, if she were to "go in for" all this, she would simply be playing a 'feminine role' (or, worse, a feminine role thrust on her 'by society') could hardly have reflected very seriously upon the concepts in question.

Most of these points can be stated without coming down on one side or the other in the matter of basic sex differences—although I have spoken of 'men' and 'women.' There are some corollaries. The person who accepts the power of passive beauty (as few people do in practice) will not only accept but welcome a good many things that tend to alarm both men and women; although in rather different ways. If (and our abhorrence of such language is perhaps a measure of our denial) you see yourself as a delightful, mysterious, exciting object, like a garden or a city into which the other has strayed, then you will want all sorts of things, some of which are alarming. You will want not only to be admired, marvelled at, and worshipped from afar and not only to offer the other such enjoyments as you think are acceptable and safe and that preserve your dignity but also to be thoroughly enjoyed, used, stretched to the full, and turned inside out. Some of this is alarming (and it is easy to see how this alarm turns quickly into a defensive attitude that uses words like 'degrading'); but your power is precisely coentensive with your vulnerability, the treasure only as valuable in use as you have courage to unlock the doors and let it be handled.

The fact that images of this kind have, traditionally, been applied to women rather than to men is really irrelevant here. If it is something that women can see and want in men, as well as vice versa, excellent: so many the more chances of enjoyment for all, and any man who refused to let himself be seen and used in such a way would have an inappropriate concept of dignity. Most of the contents of our concepts of dignity, as of 'honor' and 'integrity' (discussed earlier), are often designed to keep certain fears at bay. The only way out of this lies in appreciating that if beauty makes one vulnerable, it also makes one powerful—that if it is something that can be neglected or abused or trampled on, the abuse lies in the fears and misperceptions of the other and constitutes no real threat to oneself. The person who is secure in this knowledge, man or woman, is likely both to give and receive more in the erotic life than any other sort of person.

NOTES

I have tried throughout this book to restrain myself from undue and extended discussion, still more from polemic, about what particular representatives of the feminist movement have said or written. However, it is important to see just how, and how badly, things go wrong when politics and human feelings, entirely natural and understandable in themselves, corrupt philosophy. I permit myself one example: see M. Frye, "Male Chauvinism," in *Philosophy and Sex*, ed. Robert Baker and Frederick Elliston (Buffalo, N. Y.: Prometheus, 1975), pp. 67-68, 79. Frye has this to say:

> Sexists are those who hold certain sorts of general beliefs about sexual differences and their consequences. They hold beliefs that would, for instance, support the view that physical differences between the sexes must always make for significant social and economic differences. [So far, so good: I think I believe that.] In many cases, of course, these general beliefs might more accurately be represented by the simple proposition: Males are innately superior to females. [Now something funny has happened: why does she think that believing in *differences* has any connection or overlap with believing in *superiority*?]

We continue:

> One kind of sexist is one who shares this attitude [namely, that his beliefs are falsifiable] with respect to the epistemological status of such beliefs and differs from the feminist primarily in taking one version or another of them to be true, while the feminist holds that all such theories are false. I call this person a *doctrinaire sexist*. [Her italics: but they might be mine, since if *doctrinaire* means anything plausible at all, it would be better applied to someone who "holds that *all* such theories are false."]

There is a disarming if muddling footnote here:

> It should be noted that such theories are sexist only if they are false: for if true, they would not count as marking the sexes irrelevantly or impertinently. [I am not sure what *impertinently* means here, but I hope it is just a pleonasm for *irrelevantly*, since presumably we are concerned with truth rather than good manners.] Consequently my own use of the terms "sexist" and "sexism" in connection with such theories constitutes a certain commitment in this regard. [Now, I am a bit lost: does *sexist* mean "one who holds beliefs (of the relevant kind) that M. Frye thinks to be false" or "one who holds beliefs and so on that *are* in fact false (whatever M. Frye thinks)," or what? This all seems a good *reductio ad absurdum* argument for the uselessness of the term.]

But never mind: so far I think I am a "doctrinaire sexist," but now: "There is another kind of sexist who would cheerfully assent to the same sorts of sexist propositions as those accepted by the doctrinaire sexist but who does not view them as mere theories. Such people, whom I call *primitive sexists* are committed to these propositions as a priori truth." Now I think I am a primitive sexist, since I do not think the propositions, or all the propositions, are strictly empirical. Some seem, if true, conceptually true, which is fairly close to a priori.

2. John Wilson, *Education in Religion and the Emotions* (London: Heinemann, 1971), Pt. 2 and apps.

3. *Iliad*, 6. 490-93.

4. See, for instance, A. Ferguson, "Androgyny as an Ideal for Human Development," in *Feminism and Philosophy*, ed. Mary Vetterling-Braggin, Frederick A. Elliston, and Jane English (Totowa, N. J.: Littlefield, Adams, 1977).

9

EQUALITY, WANTS, AND INTERESTS

Some feminists who speak of a "male-dominated society" or any other groups or individuals who complain of being dominated (not being given a fair deal or a fair crack of the whip or not being treated justly or as equals) commonly conflate two quite different problems. One of them is philosophical, and the other of them at least has important philosophical aspects: but they are different. There is one sense in which such groups tend to understate their claim and in which justice has certainly not been done to their position even by the most liberally minded philosophers. There is also another sense in which the claim is overstated and much more disputable (indeed, in its doctrinaire forms, obviously absurd).

In this chapter I deal only with the first problem, which may fairly be classed under the heading of 'equality'. Nobody supposes that people are equally X, where X stands for some empirical characteristic that is capable of degree: people are more or less strong, wise, intelligent, brave, and even (something once firmly believed but now unfashionable) good at ruling. But moral and political philosophy has long been concerned with the idea that people are or ought to be, morally and politically, ultimately on an equal footing: that, in default of special circumstances, they have an equal right to consideration, or making up the rules, or to happiness—that one person's interests have no particular priority over another's. I am concerned primarily here with what, elsewhere,[1] I have called equality of *scope*—that is, with the idea of people being equal partners in setting up some system. This must surely be of primary importance: it is making up the rules of the game that matters—what might be called equality of *treatment* is a subordinate notion, a function of what the rules are in the first place.

Suppose that there is a good reason to believe that women are much better off (as Aristotle seems to have believed) when being ruled, rather like young children. Suppose that this genuinely suits them and is in their best interests. Then it would no doubt be wise for them to appreciate this and count themselves lucky if they lived in a society that had such a regime (instead of being forced into positions of ruling that, on this supposition, do not suit them). Suppose also that this regime is, ultimately, upheld by force (or some form of conditioning, indoctrination, or whatever). Is it reasonable to object *simply* on the grounds that the force is there, *not* on the grounds that the regime is against feminine interest? Can we say, for instance, that a woman is reasonably entitled to follow her own wants and options (which may include ruling) and must not be presented (browbeaten, and so on) even in her own interests? I think we can: and this is what I meant by saying that the feminist claim about "male domination" was in one way too weak, for force or nonrational persuasion would be unreasonable even if in the interests of women.

The basic question here is among the most venerable problems of moral and political philosophy, and I approach it with trepidation, encouraged only by the fact that some aspects of it at least seem not to have been squarely faced. Part of the trouble is that philosophers sometimes seem to take for granted a picture in which there is *already* a 'we' (or a "State")[2] who decides what is good for people or determines the (to *some* extent indeterminate) concepts of 'harm', 'interests', 'interference', or whatever. It is precisely this picture to which some people object (often very forcefully or irrationally) on the grounds that such things should be settled by *agreement*, neither imposed by any kind of force nor just accepted as "given." This idea lies *behind* much philosophical writing in which the concept of interests seems often to be taken as the only proper basis for action. Thus, even extreme 'liberals' or 'prescriptivists' are prepared to say things like "Most of us, indeed, think that drug addicts can legitimately be put under some restraint. We think that this is legitimate in the interests of the addict."[3] This basis is, at least, questionable. It needs to be contrasted with a basis that gives primacy to what people (in an appropriate sense) *want* or *opt for*.

This sense survives various moves that I may make, recognizing that I am weak-willed, or uninformed, or stupid, or reasonable, or inexperienced. Thus, I might say to my doctor (wife, government), "Look, I am hopelessly ignorant about medicine (cooking, economics): I hereby grant you the right to decide for me." Or I might say, "I am hopelessly weak-willed about smoking, but my settled policy is to stop: so I hereby grant you the right to hide my cigarettes." In both these cases what I want, in our sense, is wholly preserved, for I have granted a mandate. If I have not granted a mandate, I may resent certain things that my neighbors do, if they turn out not to be in line with my policy: and I shall certainly resent their arrogating the right to decide for me. The same point applies if my doctor (wife, government) claims the right to act in my interests or my 'best interests'—that is, if he claims the right to do what he thinks is good for me. I shall feel that he only has the right if I *give* it to him. He may act in my interests if, but only if, I have empowered him so to act.

If, owing to failure in communication, or lack of time, or some other contingent difficulty, I have neither empowered him nor refused to empower him, then I shall want him to act by the criterion of what (given a proper state of communication) I *would* have chosen—that is, whether I would have so empowered him or not. For instance, if my wife is uncertain about whether to hide my cigarettes, she should settle the question not by whether it is in my interests to smoke or whether (in some *other* sense) I want to smoke but by whether I would empower her to decide the question for me. In this example she has only to ask. There are many cases, particularly in politics, where bad communications make the answer harder. But this should be the criterion for answering.

I am not sure what theories of the kind found in the works of John Rawls[4] or R. M. Hare[5] would say about this, because it is not clear to me that they bring this particular point out into the open. They would agree, probably, that the criterion must be either what a person would "prescribe" or "contract for" if he was to be asked (or if I put myself in his shoes) or what he does in fact prescribe or contract for if he has in fact been asked. But there is the possibility of one or the other, or both, of two additional implications, both of which have to be resisted. The implications are (1) that the person must be in possession of all or some of the available facts relating to his own interests and (2) that those facts must guide him in his prescription and contract making. It might be thought that these can be collapses, since what is the point of (1) being aware of relevant facts if (2) the person is not going to be guided by them? Actually they are importantly different, as some further examples will show—examples that I hope will also make clearer what I mean by "a proper state of communication" in the previous paragraph.

John Stuart Mill's bridge-crossing case, perhaps the most difficult type of case for advocates of the "wants" criterion, may occur to us here. I see a man about to cross a bridge that I know, but he perhaps does not, to be dangerous: there being no time for communication as between equals, do I have the right to prevent him by force? There is a slight air of unreality about this example, since nothing may prevent me from temporarily detaining the man in conversation—I just have to say, "Hi! That bridge is dangerous!"; and even the most ardent advocate of personal freedom will hardly object to such an encroachment on a man's time. But now suppose I am the benevolent ruler of a backward people who, for whatever reasons, wish to throw me and my wise colleagues out of their country. I should like to say, "Wait a minute, let me explain why this will be disastrous to you: all the competent doctors and scientists and judges will go; you will have plague and not much food and corrupt justice and civil war"—and I would want quite a lot of time to educate them so that they saw this for themselves (by which time, perhaps, they could manage by themselves anyway). Now, can I reasonably force (browbeat, and so on) them to give me this time on the grounds that only this allows "a proper state of communication"?

There are various attitudes that this backward people might adopt (A^1) They might simply refuse to listen. (A^2) They might deny or be uncertain about the facts. (B) They might accept the facts but still (against their interests) opt that I and my colleagues should quit the country. It seems to me that (A^1) and (A^2) corespond to (1) above, and (B) to (2)—that is, we might feel ourselves entitled to demand either (1) that they listened and learned the facts and/or (2) that their options or prescriptions were guided by them. If we make no attempt to communicate, but simply ask ourselves what their prescriptions would be, this makes no difference, for either we put ourselves in their shoes *with* either or both the implications, (1) and (2), or *without* them. Similarly, to go back to the smoking example, and assuming that my wife either has or can grab my cigarettes, she might think it necessary (1) that I know the key facts about smoking and health and/or (2) that I opt in the light of these facts which would, other things being equal, result in an option against smoking, which is damaging to health.

These implications ought themselves to be subject to contractual negotiation. That is, I (you, he, anyone) may be the sort of person to say to my wife (or to an occupying colonial power) something like, "Look, if you think I am doing something gravely against my interests, I grant you a mandate to stop me by force while we discuss it for, say, and hour: after that we will do another deal. But I do not grant you a mandate to use any more force—not even if I myself agree that it is against my interests to do whatever I am doing. There are times, perhaps many times, when I want to be allowed to go to hell in my own way." This might, in other words, be what I *would in fact prescribe*: now it should be clear how the "wants" criterion can override these implications about interests and factual knowledge. If we all agree that we should know the facts and act in our own interests *and* that other people can legitimately stop us when these conditions are not satisfied, fine—but if not, not. Few would probably agree to all of this in a blank-check kind of way, although many might agree to *some* forcible encroachment on their time for purposes of explanation and *some* degree of other uses of force (for example, as in the bridge-crossing case, where there is immediate danger to life or limb). In any case, what matters is their actual or predicted agreement, whatever their state of ignorance or irrationality.

I have not as yet given anything approaching an *argument* for preferring the "wants" criterion; I have tried only to clarify what it is. At least if we now ask, "Should we act in accordance with other people's wants or in accordance with their interests?" we can at once see that the context of the question is crucial. For if 'we' already have, in some areas or to some extent, mandatory powers to act in other people's interests, the advocate of the 'wants' criterion has no quarrel. If 'we' do not have such powers, he will complain of imposition and interference. If "drug addicts can legitimately be put under some restraints" because "we think that this is legitimate *in the interests of the addict*," the "wants" advocate will at least require to know what people, with what powers, 'we' refers to and what is meant by 'legitimately'. Another writer says:

> Mill carried his protest against paternalism to lengths that may now appear to us fantastic. He cites the example of restrictions of the sale of drugs, and criticizes them as interferences. . . . if we no longer sympathize with this criticism this is due, in part, to a general decline in the belief that individuals know their own interests best, and to an increased awareness of a great range of factors which diminish the significance to be attached to an apparently free choice or to consent.[6]

But who are "we"? And have 'we' all agreed, *at an earlier stage*, that in some predetermined cases where people do not 'know their own interests best' or where their choice is only 'apparently free' that there wants should be overridden?

In practice the members of most societies have made no such agreement: there was not (empirically) any such contract.[7] But if the advocate of the "wants" criterion is to be satisfied, we must go back—in logic and by communication, if not in time—to this prior stage; otherwise there seems to be no ultimate defense against the objectionable imposition of other criteria. Such criteria may, notoriously, be of very different kinds but all operate by excluding some classes of people, so that what those classes want does not count. Thus, we may exclude children, morons, women, non-Aryans, the senile, the stupid, criminals, and so on. We may do this in one of two ways: either we know or guess beforehand what they will want, disapprove of it, and, therefore, disqualify them; or we disqualify them on the more general grounds that they are irrational, inexperienced, and so on. To the advocate of the "wants" criterion either move is unjustified, for, again, who are the "we"? If these classes of people agree (want, contract) to disqualify themselves, there is no problem; if they do not, then 'we' (the others) have no right to force them. There is only one class of people that the "wants" criterion excludes: the class of people (if one may call them people) who do not have wants in the required sense. This might exclude very young children and others too moronic or too lunatic to hold or express anything we could reasonably call an option or a settled policy. It would not exclude, however, many who would be excluded by some other criterion: for instance, normal 15-year-olds.

I hope this is sufficient at least to show that there *is* a problem and that one might be considerably worried by an over-causual reliance on "interests." Whatever the solution, it seems important that we should carefully consider what I have called the "first stage"—the stage of communication or negotiation logically antecedent to the acceptance of any particular deals: as for instance with two strangers on an otherwise desert island. It is clear that in practice the crucial moves of this stage are procedural: some preliminary agreement has to be reached about the terms of negotiation.

This is not the place to attempt a full-scale defense of the notion of negotiation, considered as a requirement of pure reason; but it may be worth advancing some considerations that seem to bear upon it. One (anyone) is in a world where there are all sorts of different individuals and social groups with different principles and outlooks. Some might be out purely for their own interests; others might not be concerned with *interests* at all. In the first stage of one's dealings with others, one cannot fairly *start by* laying down a particular substantive principle or moral theory, however much may be said for the theory in point of pure reason. For this would not be just nor offer a fair basis for negotiation: what may be said for the theory will have to be said only after negotiation is under way. In other words, we—that is, two strangers—have to start with a blank sheet as regards *any* particular views. We have to foreswear force and imposition *before* dealing with any particular issue. Our initial move has to be something like "We agree to discuss, debate, and (possibly) decide issues by such-and-such procedures, whatever views may triumph"; and we have to universalize this as, "One ought to agree to. . . ." and so on. Moral theories themselves are among the things that have to be shelved if we are to operate by discussion and negotiation rather than by force or imposition. The only alternative to this is to commit oneself to the principle: One ought only to negotiate on the basis of one's own moral theory, which is, in effect, not to negotiate at all in the required sense.

The question can no doubt be raised But why negotiate in the first place? We could try to meet this by quoting the contingent merits of the practice: we are all apt to make mistakes, we need the help of other men in discussion to clarify our views and discover the truth, most of us wish to establish some definitive principle that will avoid tyranny, and so on. But we may still seek for some logically compelling argument. Negotiation is not always possible (with madmen, invading Nazis, and so on); but if someone were to say that, when possible, it was not reasonable and desirable, I think we should find this hard to understand. Given that there are or may be conflicting interests, moral and political theories, ideals, and so on, and that we wish for or cannot avoid some form of human interaction, to what other general principle could a reasonable man commit himself? The alternative to negotiation, where there is no unanimity, is some kind of war. Of course, a man may find it easy to believe that war is to be preferred to negotiation in a particular case—that is, if he thinks that his outlook will survive war but may not survive negotiation.

But on what grounds would he believe that *in general* war is the right way to settle such issues? Certainly a man could *say*, "One ought always to fight it out," but what reason could he give for this? The point is that what he cannot rationally do is to accept the merits of negotiation except when *he* thinks otherwise. To adapt Hare's famous example, the relevant question is not just How would you like it if you were on the receiving end of your own outlook? (that is, be put into a gas chamber if you were a Jew) but, How would you like it if the Jews were in power, held an ideal about an Aryan-free world, and put you into a gas chamber on those grounds? The 'fanatic' has to universalize not only in respect to his own ideal but also in respect to the legitimacy or illegitimacy of anyone imposing any ideal. He has to face the question (since this question can arise at the 'first stage')[8] Are we going to impose ideals on each other or are we not? If there are good reasons that a person could offer for accepting the principle that one (anyone) ought to impose one's (anyone's) ideals, I cannot see what they are.

Whatever the force of these considerations, it is important to be clear that the thesis undercuts a picture common in much contemporary philosophy, in which (to put it briefly) there are supposed to be a number of independent 'principles' or 'values' that do not stand in any hierarchical relationship. Thus, R. S. Peters would justify the "framework of order" needed for education not "under the principle of liberty" but "under the principle of the promotion of what is good, with its subordinate principle of the consideration of what is in people's interests";[9] and later, "As, however, freedom is an independent principle like justice it cannot be abrogated entirely for the sake of the promotion of what is good. The presumption in favor of it still holds."[10] Our thesis, on the other hand, maintains that some sort of negotiation or contract is logically prior to, and should determine, any publicly-enforced concept of "what is good" or "people's interests." Even if this were not so, our problem would still be a worrying one: for if 'freedom' were an "independent principle" (whatever this may mean), how would we know *when* to "abrogate" it "for the sake of the promotion of what is good"? We can hardly say (though Peters implies this)[11] that 'we' are entitled to abrogate it whenever 'we' feel sure that our case is a good one—this gives the individual no ultimate defense against tyranny. At the very least, we need clear criteria for when we are entitled to abrogate and when we are not. This drives us back to the thesis according to which such criteria ought themselves to be the result of negotiation rather than imposition.

I have tried to make it as clear as possible just what the issue is here, because there is another issue with which it may be confused and about which there is already a good deal of literature. This may be roughly described under the heading of "liberal" (or "democratic") *methods or regimes*. A brief word about this is in order here, if only to see that it is different from our own problem.

Political movements that might be called "liberal," "democratic," "anti-authoritarian," and so on, may be concerned with some of the same phenomena that might worry a contract theorist: for instance, the raising of the compulsory school-leaving age or women not being allowed to vote or being forced into certain roles (for example, housekeeping). The advocated 'solution' is that we should run schools and families and other institutions in a more 'liberal' or 'democratic' way. The 'regime' of the institution or the 'methods' or 'approach' of teachers and males should be less 'authoritarian'; and the view seems to be that this will give us all we need by way of liberty and justice.

We need first to distinguish between two positions that might be termed 'liberal'. The distinction emerges in this example: In one marriage (A^1) the partners' relationships are Miltonic or Victorian. Generally, the man commands and his wife obeys. In another (A^2) they share in the day-to-day decision making: we might say, they operate as equals. However, we are to assume that in both these cases the two partners have *negotiated* their relationships. In A^1 the wife has *agreed* to obey and the husband to command; in A^2 both have agreed to share the decision making. Imagine two other marriages, B^1 and B^2: these are outwardly similar to A^1 and A^2 but there has been no negotiation. In B^1 the husband has simply arrogated the right to command and/or the wife, the role of obedience; in B^2 each just takes—without prior agreement—a proportion of the decisions.

When we talk of people holding a 'liberal' point of view toward other people or of their "respecting them as persons," "considering their interests," "granting them equality," and so on, we may be interested in one of two things. We may be interested in their general behavior patterns: in A^1 these are 'illiberal', 'unequal', 'authoritarian', in A^2, the opposite. We may be interested in whether these behavior patterns were negotiated (agreed, contractually accepted) or otherwise. Here the distinction is not between 1 and 2 but between A and B. In A, both (very different) types of behavior patterns were negotiated; in B, neither.

If when we talk of 'liberty', 'equality', and so on, we are interested in the first of these distinctions—that is, in what I have called the "general behavior patterns"—then it is clear that liberals in *this* sense must hold an empirical thesis. They must believe that human nature is such or that a particular society is such—that a liberal (in this sense) behavior pattern is most suitable for those concerned. If, for instance, they are in favor of marriages with 'equality rela-tionships', they must hold that men and women are, as a matter of fact, such that these relationships and not others bring them the most happiness or are best for them. If it turned out, for instance, that most women were much happier, saner, better off (or whatever criteria may be used) when, in general, they are told what to do by men, then this liberal thesis would fail.

Certain conclusions are already obvious. First, it seems that any very *general* thesis of liberalism in this sense would be suicidal. To suggest that a liberal structure for life or 'equality relationships' suits *all* people, irrespective of age, sex, political development, or emotional maturity, appears now as a gro-tesquely arrogant (because factually unsupported) claim. Perhaps arguments might be advanced to show that such a regime *ought* to suit everyone, even if it does not: but it is hard to see what such arguments would look like, and in any case it still leaves the thesis dependent on psychological, political, and many other kinds of fact. Further, some contexts (for example, war) will clearly demand particular regimes that are very different from those required by other contexts (for example, a philosophy seminar).

Second, since the distinction between 1 and 2 is very different from A and B, it is clear that a regime may be extremely liberal in one sense and extremely illiberal in another. Go back to example A_1: suppose the wife has said something to the effect of, "George, I hate making decisions, and I would be much happier if you told me what to do (even though I may sometimes complain): so what I opt for, on my part, is a regime whereby I do what I am told." And, now suppose the husband says, "No, my dear, I am going to insist that you do your share of the decision making: I think it is good for you, and, anyway, I hate giving orders." If he wins, the resulting regime appears liberal and, indeed, is so in sense 1; but it is no longer liberal in sense A—it has been imposed, as in the B case.

Third, a point made earlier but worth repeating: in the example just given the husband quoted the wife's interests as a reason for an 'equality relationship', and in other examples a person may quote another's interests as a reason for a quite different, 'authoritarian' relationship. So it is clear that the second (more basic) type of liberalism—that is, A as against B, negotiation as against imposition—*has nothing to do with accepting others' interests as a criterion.* What distinguishes A from B is not that the A-liberal is concerned with others' interests, whereas the B-liberal does not care about them. The difference is this: that the A-liberal does not count his concerns—even his concern for what he thinks is good for other people—as having any more weight than the other person's.

This is why I have described the difference in terms like 'negotiated', 'agreed', 'opt for', and 'contractually accepted'. What weights with the A-type liberal is not what is (in his view) good for the other, or what is in the other's interests, but what the other wants or opts for. This is to remain true whether the other's option is for a 'liberal' (in sense 1) or an 'authoritarian' regime. The liberal in sense A will admit that the regime reached as a result of bargaining or collating options may be unwise, lunatic, or even suicidal. But if he is a liberal in this sense, he will maintain that this is how things ought to be decided in the last resort—that is, unless and until we have already passed the 'first stage' of basic negotiation and agreed to entrust decision making to some other process (a kind, or a parliament, or a body of elders, or whatever authority we undertake to accept).

I stress this because it is very important to grasp that the *terms* of any contract or deal that may be made are quite a different matter from whether there actually is any contract or deal. As a matter of empirical fact we are often not in a position to know (or even make plausible guesses) about what individual negotiators would—after due reflection and experience—opt for, since only rarely are their options even canvassed, let alone enforced. We know well enough, for instance, what regimes pupils appear to *like* in schools or what TV programs are *popular*; but because pupils and TV viewers are in the position of consumers rather than negotiators, these do not necessarily represent their considered options. A question often phrased as something like, 'Should the viewing public be given what they want or what is good (culturally improving, et cetera) for them?' misses the point: what we want to know is, 'Would the viewing public opt for a policy for TV that produces only popular programs or one that is also governed by other criteria?' It is wrong to assume that an individual's option will necessarily be for his "ground-level" wants. Similarly, pupils might, particularly after some experience, come to opt for much more stringent discipline than their 'ground-level' reactions might suggest. Cloudy notions like 'participation' and 'democracy' mask this essential distinction, which has an obvious relevance not only to education and feminism but to political questions in general.

A great deal has been written about the notion of "rational" authority, and I do not want to convey the impression that it is a waste of time to get clear about this in education and other areas. Faced with the phenomena of unrest, hostility, rebellion, 'liberation' movements, and so on, of course, "the proper reaction should not be the abandonment of the claim to authority but the rationalization of it."[12] But this is not enough. Most philosophical discussion is concerned with the question of what sort of authority, rules, institutions, aims, and so on, "reasonable men" would accept. But when we are clear about this, we are clear only about something we can reasonably *offer* to individuals, not about something we can reasonably *impose* on them. If all pupils, all males and females, were "reasonable men," we should have no problem. Since they are not—though it is worth remembering that there may be occasions when they are "reasonable" and "we" are not—we have to take the business of negotiation seriously.

There are deeper causes for our refusal to face the problem squarely. One common notion is that there is something rather nasty or brutal about contracts or 'deals' and that we can avoid all this by having and deploying enough 'concern' or "love" or 'reasonableness'—a fantasy beloved by tender-minded liberals, as a kind of counterweight to the 'authoritarian' fantasy that 'we' so obviously know what is best for other people that the whole idea of negotiation is absurd. Another obstacle is the immense size and difficulty of the task of negotiation. If we accept (as I think we must) that without appropriate mandates we do not have rights of enforcement, all problems of this kind can only be resolved by achieving greater political clarity about particular cases. This entails getting clear, by practical communication with those involved, precisely where the various parties stand—having clear and just formulations of their options and mandates and having contracts plainly spelled out. This is a daunting task, and there are naturally many reasons why we shirk it: the size and complexity of modern society, simple intertia, the vague wish to let sleeping dogs lie, the desire to make partisan capital out of the situation precisely by leaving it ambiguous, the fantasy that there is already some sort of contract when there is not, or even perhaps the very deep-rooted dislike of clarification in general—particularly when this leads to the operation of rules and sanctions rather than of "general goodwill," "common sense," "what all reasonable people subscribe to," and so forth.

The more overtly political aspects of this are particularly regrettable. Often "we" are somehow just assumed to have rights of enforcement, or there is taken to be some 'general consensus', or matters are left to the pushes and pulls of various interest groups (sometimes this last is called 'democracy'). What makes so much of practical politics tedious for the rational man is that very little attempt is made even to discover (let alone realize) the options of various individuals and groups: events are adjusted and pressures yielded to *ad hoc*, without much regard for justice or wisdom. The authorities, understandably enough, appear chiefly anxious to keep things quiet and on an even keel. It is, for instance, difficult not to believe that the comparative political impotence of 15-year-old adolescents, as against the trouble-making power of university and other students, has something to do with the stringent compulsions applied to the former as against the almost unbelievable license granted to the latter. The combination of a failure to achieve and enforce clear contracts plus the willingness to yield to pressure is a standing invitation to any group that wants its own way.

The version of the contract thesis that I have been advancing offers no simple and short-term solution. This, though it may disappoint, is surely something in its favor. Much of the task of canvassing and collating options ought in principle to have been accomplished long ago *pari passu* with the establishing of various institutions and relationships in society. It is easy to see why it has been neglected and leaves us with an immense amount of work to do. The thesis points only to the kind of work that needs doing: to get back (in communication, since we cannot in time) to the first stage and negotiate it. However daunting or unreal this may seem, I do not think that anyone who sympathizes with the thesis will find it hard to think of many practical moves that could be made almost immediately.

There are political problems in the sense that their effective solution demands collective, not only individual, action. What I want to bring out here, as elsewhere, is the extent to which intelligent action depends on the rejection of fantasy. It is much easier to treat them 'politically' in a more degraded sense: that is, to identify oneself with, or attempt some compromise between, various interest groups—those who shout for "more discipline," "a return to decency," "standards," or "liberation" or institutionalized groups such as the women's and men's liberation movements and black power. Or, we may identify enemies under titles such as 'alienation', 'apathy', 'the establishment', 'male chauvinists', 'viragos', and 'revolutionaries.' To pay serious attention to the options of other people demands even harder work than to pay serious attention to their interests; we have to substitute a process of communication and agreement for processes that involve the imposition of our own first-order values, however (apparently) high-minded these may be. (A philosophically fashionable and tender-minded 'liberalism', lacking in nerve because it is fearful of its own unconscious aggression and, hence, reluctant to make realistic and tough-minded "deals" with women, children, and others, is among the fantasies that we have to reject.)

I am not claiming that there could be no serious philosophical disagreement with the contract thesis. One might follow some philosophers[13] in maintaining that it is quite unworrisome (or perhaps inevitable) that sovereign states should wish to promote certain ideals for their citizens and employ coercion for this purpose: so that, provided a majority of people in our society wished to force an ideal of 'being educated' on everybody, a minority of objectors can with propriety be coerced. But this seems far too lighthearted an approach, for (1) we do not *know* whether a majority of people support this ideal or think it right to enforce it; (2) it is unclear whether such people would be willing to universalize with respect to imposing ideals in the way I have argued that it is necessary if the imposition of this ideal is to pass one test of reason; and (3) even then there seems little harm and much good in allowing those who disagree to opt out of these particular social demands where possible. From these and similar points I wish chiefly to single out the first (1). Without wanting to cut short any philosophical debate, one may fairly point out that we live in a pluralistic and uncertain society, where we find difficulty in clarifying and enforcing even the most minimal contracts. Let us at least begin with this: it will be time enough later on to consider whether we wish also to enforce ideals.

NOTES

1. John Wilson, *Equality* (London: Hutchinson, 1966).
2. John R. Lucas, *Principles of Politics* (Oxford: Oxford University Press, 1966), pp. 167 ff., 292 ff., 341 ff.
3. Richard M. Hare, *Freedom and Reason* (Oxford: Oxford University Press, 1963), p. 174.
4. John Rawls, *A Theory of Justice* (Oxford: Oxford University Press, 1972).
5. Hare, *Freedom and Reason*; idem, *Philosophical Quarterly* 23 (1973); and idem, "Ethical Theory and Utilitariansim," in *Contemporary British Philosophy*, ed. H. D. Lewis, vol. 3, (Atlantic Highlands, N.J.: Humanities Press, 1977).
6. H. L. Hart, *Law, Liberty and Morality* (Oxford University Press, 1963), pp. 32-33.
7. It is curious enough that philosophers continue to regard arguments as "enough to discredit the Contract theory" (Lucas, *Principles of Politics*): that (1) there never was a contract, (2) even if there had been it would need constant reendorsement, and (3) you cannot spell out all the details in in advance. But all any sensible "Contract theorist" contends is that (1) there ought to be one, (2) it ought to be constantly reendorsed, and (3) as much

should be spelled out as is possible or reasonable. The objection (4) that "if consent is a necessary condition of political obligation, it would deny a government any rightful authority over anyone who dissented from the basic principles of the constitution" (S. Benn and R.S. Peters, *Social Theory and the Democratic State* [Winchester, Mass.: Allen & Unwin, 1959], p. 322) does not seem to me an objection at all but rather a restatement of the contract thesis. "No one who chose to contract out could be legitimately coerced" (idem, *Social Theory and the Democratic State.*) Just so and quite right, too. Questions about who shall be allowed to contract out, on what occasions, for what reasons, at what times, et cetera should themselves be subject to prior negotiation and contract. Anthony Quinton (*Introduction to Political Philosophy* [Oxford: Oxford University Press, 1967], p. 12) mentions "Hume's favorite objection that the good ends for which the promise was made are sufficient to justify obedience to the state by themselves and without the intermediary of a highly speculative act of moral commitment. This leads to the conceptually more economical view of *utilitarianism*, that obedience to the state is justified on directly teleological grounds as a necessary condition of the general welfare, the advantage of society at large." This is a muddle. There are questions about what deals/contracts we would be wise to make ("for good ends" or "on teleological grounds") but quite different questions about what deals/contracts we do make, or have made, or would (if asked) make. It is precisely this distinction that the contract theorist wants to insist on.

8. B.A. Williams, "Egoism and Altrusim," in *Problems of the Self* (Cambridge: Cambridge University Press, 1973). The egoist is confronted by questions, surely intelligible, about what principles of procedure or behavior it would be most reasonable (wise, sensible, et cetera) for men in general to adopt. If he denied sense to such questions, or thought that one answer was as good another, I think we should say that he was not even trying to be rational about it. Equally his own desires seem to have no logical relevance to such questions: how to bring them into line with what is reasonable is a separate matter. Williams, perhaps, allows this (p. 257). See also John Wilson, *Education in Religion and the Emotions* (London: Heinemann, 1971), pp. 217 ff.; also my reply to F. Dunlop in idem, *Proceedings of the Philosophy of Education Society of Great Britain* 11 (1972): 98ff.; idem, *A Preface to the Philosophy of Education* (Boston, Mass.: Routledge & Kegan Paul, 1979).

9. R. S. Peters, *Ethics and Education* (Winchester, Mass.: Allen & Unwin, 1966), p. 194.

10. Ibid., p. 195.

11. Ibid.

12. Ibid., p. 249.

13. Lucas, *Principles of Politics*, pp. 284-301, is the clearest statement I know of.

10

POWER, INFLUENCE, AND JUSTICE

I want now to try to say something sensible about the more specific demands that women or feminists might make, other than the demand (already conceded—indeed, hotly argued for—in the last chapter) for an equality of scope —that is, an equal voice in making up the rules, an equal weight attached to their options (*not* what other people, nor even themselves, think to be in their interests). The main difficulty here is to steer clear, though perhaps not too clear, of the purely empirical. What actual positions, regimes, types of power or influence, roles, jobs, et cetera that suit women (or anybody else) is chiefly an empirical matter. That women should, in the sense described earlier, be regarded as equals seems to me not in dispute, but what counts as *doing justice* to women, apart from this, is highly debatable. The best we can hope for here is to clear the decks for an unbiased empirical approach and to fight free of some doctrinaire bewitchments.

We may begin with the idea of power. 'Power' is a pretty general sort of word and partly for that reason is apt to be interpreted in too specific terms. Some sort of distinction can be made between political power and other sorts (for instance, being 'powerfully built')—but even this is far from easy, probably because we are not clear as to what is to count as politics and how to demarcate this from other enterprises or areas. 'Social power' is vaguer still, as is most talk about 'society'. We might raise the question, Who had the most power over what happened in states and cities (*poleis*), Hitler or Jesus or Einstein? and be uncertain about how to answer, although if we asked, Who held most *political* power? we would probably opt for Hitler. Political power, we might say as a sighting shot, is power held in virtue of some *authorization* by the state or society. It is because someone is officially the dictator, or president, or mayor, or whatever, that whatever power he uses in that office is political, which might distinguish it, roughly, from military power, charismatic power, influence, or other such things (whatever they are).

Quite a large number of cases come somewhere between political power and influence: 'social power' might (vaguely) entitle these. There might be one complaint about whether women had enough political power and another question about whether they were accepted as "leaders of society" or as having some other kind of power—particularly economic power—that gave them a fair measure of control *in a social context*. The difficulty of drawing this distinction is the difficulty of determining what is to count as "social" or "society." We would be able to distinguish, perhaps, the case of someone who had great influence on various individuals in their nonsocial aspects—for example, Jane Austen, or Madame Curie, or Montessori—from the case of someone who exercised direct power or control over them socially—for example, some leader of fashion, or the president of an economically powerful corporation, or Lucrezia Borgia. Not that the former sort of person would not 'influence society' but only indirectly (like Jesus or the Buddah), whereas political power, and (more vaguely) 'social power', act directly on people's social economic aspects. Aspasia, Pericles's mistress, no doubt had an important influence on Athenian politics when Pericles was elected general; this, however, is importantly different from herself being so elected.

All this is distressingly vague but perhaps sufficient to see that there are a number of very different kinds of power. No doubt in practice they interlock, and theories have been produced to show that some one kind is central (for instance, Marxism and economic power). But if anyone were to say that there were *no* distinctions to be made here, that there was just some *one thing* called 'power in society' (or even some one thing called 'society'), he would be simply making matters worse. Clearly, we want to differentiate between the effects of Hitler, Jesus, and Einstein or between Queen Elizabeth I, Saint Theresa, and Madame Curie. Someone who said, for instance, that they were all products of a certain kind of economic system might, indeed, have something to say, but not something helpful for differentiating closely between various kinds of power and influence.

The reason why we need to differentiate is so that we can lay out at least a number of tolerably clear options or *kinds* of 'effect'. Somebody deciding what to do with his life must decide, if only in ignorance or tacitly, between these, since it is unlikely that he will have the time, talent, or opportunity to take on all the options at once, some of them being virtually full-time jobs. The problem is by no means unique to feminism: there are questions about whether I can (am allowed to, ought to, have the capacity to) be a writer or a businessman, just as there are questions about whether I can be a mother of six or a businesswoman. It is only when we have laid out at least some options that we can confront other questions, in particular the two questions What effects (power, influence) ought people be allowed to have? and What effects (et cetera) are worth having?

So far as the first of these questions is concerned, even the most ardent anti-feminist must surely concede that the criterion of competence (interpreted in a sufficiently broad sense) would be by far the most important. If there is a vacancy for a job, for instance, then presumably we want the best person for the job—man, woman, black, white or Martian. Naturally, it might be argued (indeed, it seems to be not only argued but actually practiced in some quarters) that political desirability should to some extent be allowed to override competence: that—to take a nonemotive example—unless we actually insist on some quota of Martians in certain jobs or positions of power, Martians will be viewed prejudicially. This may, in certain cases, be true. But, if we are talking about what ideally ought to happen, we are entitled at least to imagine a society in which unreasonable prejudice did not operate. 'Unreasonable' here would mean, surely, that the proper criterion of competence was not adequately attended to. It would only be *because* (some) people used irrelevant reasons for their judgments that we might need to compensate politically. A sane or rational society would understand the nature of different enterprises—including politics itself—and simply want the enterprises run efficiently.

There could, therefore, be no reasonable objection to *allowing*—that is, not forbidding or discouraging by official rules or unofficial conventions—women or anyone else to attempt whatever jobs, positions, or kinds of effects they wished (meaning by "attempt," simply to try to get or 'put in for' those positions). "Because she's a woman" might be relevant to some positions or kinds of effects and might even be used as a quick, overall criterion in default of better evidence; just as, "Because he went to Oxford" is a reasonable criterion to use if it is known that I went to Oxford and am applying for a job in the slums where an Oxford accent is a severe disqualification. What women can, in fact, achieve in Mohammedan cultures is, however regrettably, limited. But no one sensibly will disqualify the application for such jobs: there may be countervailing factors, and no generalization is perfect.

It is rather the second question, What effects (kinds of power, influence, et cetera) are worth having or worth complaining about if one does not have them? that needs closer inspection. It is entirely clear that this is a very *open* question. To take an obvious example: "The hand that rocks the cradle rules the world." Now, of course, it does not, politically, rule the world, but it is perfectly plausible to say that *one* of the most important effects a person may have on human life is in child rearing. It may even be thought, as by many psychologists, that these effects (being more basic to how we think and feel) are a great deal more significant to human happiness than anything much achieved by econ-

omists, businessmen, or even politicians. Or one might hold the slightly more sophisticated view (which on the whole seems to me true) that politicians and
economists can serve us only, as it were, by keeping the ring or providing an adequate background within which what really matters can flourish—politics and
economics exist only so that we can enjoy our families, grow up happily, pursue
the arts, philosophy, or whatever takes our fancy, and generally enjoy life in a
nonpolitical way (see further below).

Did Helen of Troy have more power or influence than the male heroes of
Homer's *Iliad*? Well, even if she did, her influence was pretty disastrous. But suppose you are, like many Victorian mothers and many mothers in some contemporary societies (modern Greece might be a fair example), more or less omnip-
otent at home but virtually without power outside (we might say without
'social ' power, unless we insist on confusing the issue by saying that the family
also counts as 'society'). Is it *obviously* reasonable to react simply by saying,
"She does not have enough power"? Is it reasonable at all? Might one not react
by saying, "Frankly I am not very interested in what you call 'social' or 'political' power—nor even, since I had the sense to pick a reliable husband, 'economic'
power (though, in fact, I spend most of the wage packet): I like the sort of power I have got, thank you very much."

Much of the same point could be made by considering, what is often regarded as ammunition on the other side, various more primitive societies. It
seems to have been true in prehistoric Greece, for instance, that whereas certain
areas (fighting, hunting, organizing) were regarded as male prerogatives, certain
others—notably religion—were 'female-dominated'. Now, it is only *if* one buys
(I am tempted to say, sells out to) the view that fighting and hunting are somehow more important than religion that one will be tempted to say that in such
a society women were oppressed—just as it is only if one thinks what happens
outside the home to be more important than what happens inside it that one will
also think Victorian mothers were oppressed.

It needs to be made clear that this question is not to be settled simply by a
consideration of what is *thought*, *in* that society, to be important, not, that is,
unless one believes that social status (being thought important) is itself a good
criterion of what actually is important. This view itself at once immerses us in
the essential question of what actually is important. Such a question cannot be
divorced from one's views on human life in general. Suppose that we did, in fact,
believe that child rearing was more important than, say, being president of a
company manufacturing soap powder (not an implausible supposition), *sub spe-
cie aeternitatis*, but that owing to the idiocies of contemporary society most
people usually gave more status and prestige to soap powder makers, regarded
them as more "important," "successful," et cetera. What would one now say, if
one was a woman child rearer? Well, one would think it a pity, or tiresome, or
even thoroughly regrettable that this was so, particularly, if understandably egocentric, that one was not accorded one's due meed of status. But one would not,

surely, wish to change jobs. One would stay where one was, perhaps agitating on the side for more recognition.

Can anything further be said on this matter of importance? It seems to me a rather sad fact that, at precisely the time when economics, politics, and "social" enterprises generally have greatly diminished in importance, many people (by no means only feminists—it is a common modern disease) straitjacket a good many general notions (again, not only power) into economic and political garments. I mean this: it is plausible to say, in many societies, that we *know how to do* such things as economics and politics and even that a great deal of what those enterprises ought to do is being done. This is masked by the fact that the economic, political, and 'social' problems still remaining—and there are plenty—are for most people the most visible or salient. But we ought to face, even perhaps congratulate ourselves on, the fact that in at least some countries almost everybody has enough to eat, there are no civil wars, and people enjoy a tolerable amount of freedom.

It will immediately be said, with justice, that in many societies this is not true, that in our own and other similar ones there is plenty of crime, delinquency, ill health, and so on; and that the political and economic system falls far short of justice. Nobody denies this. I say only that the fronts on which we most urgently need to advance are not properly marked by 'economic', 'social', or even 'political' (in any narrow sense of that term). They are better marked by terms such as 'mental health', 'love', even perhaps, 'morality'. It is abundantly clear that a minimal of material prosperity is, at best, only a necessary condition for happiness: it is certainly not sufficient, and other things may be as important or more so. The chief enemy for advanced societies today, if one my be so bold with one's generalizations, is the deeply rooted fact that human beings, even if (perhaps, particularly when) they are prosperous, suffer from fantasy, unreason, neurosis, dissatisfaction, and lack of love. These are, in principle, not things that can be catered for *sociologically*, in any normal sense of that term. They are, indeed, not much to do with "society" at all: notions of a Freudian kind, or even of a Christian kind ("original sin"), or—to be fair—notions that sometimes seem to lie beneath Marxist economic and social theory, such as 'alienation', are much more in order here.

There is also the argument, which must have some force (how much would be a very hard question to answer), that even if we have economic, political, and 'social' problems—what we may call 'mass' rather than "individual" problems—we may be unable to solve them by "changing the system," or we may be unable (or unwilling) to 'change the system' unless we *first* generate enough sane and loving people to change it. It is not at all clear, to put it briefly, whether money going to developing countries should be spent on ploughshares and economists, on the one hand, or on moral educators and missionaries, on the other: it is at least arguable that, if the people always insist on beating their ploughshares into swords, the latter might be preferable. No doubt there is often a vicious circle;

we need a high-energy economy in order to educate people morally or (if one dare use the word) spiritually, but we also need people who are at least competent in morality and politics if they are to keep a high-energy economy going. This problem, or something like it, is much discussed in the context of the Protestant ethic and the rise of the middle class (notoriously in post-Renaissance Germany), without, so far as I can see, any clear solution.

Besides all the uncertainties about different kinds of power (or what is to count as 'power'), there is also the connected difficulty of allocating *fair shares* of power to the different sexes—indeed, to individuals generally. This is the most complicated problem in practical justice, partly because it is not just a philosophical problem. We need to see, though, that *equalizing* one kind of power does not necessarily produce a state of justice: not because, as has often been said (most clearly by Aristotle), people with unequal desires or needs are not justly treated if they are treated equally or the same but rather because we have to take different goods (kinds of power) into account, not just the one kind, if justice is to be done.

For example, in certain contexts (particularly, though not only, where there is a severe shortage of women or where attractive women are highly valued) simply being an attractive woman bestows a great many kinds of power. At one time in the Suez Canal Zone during the British occupation, it was reckoned worth approximately £1,000 *per annum* (in those days, a good salary itself) to be an even moderately attractive girl, if one assigned a cash value to things such as free meals, transportation, clothes, presents, jewelry, and various services. Now a girl might, of course, say that she did not want any or all of these advantages or kinds of power or that she did not want them simply by virtue of being attractive. But they existed, and a different girl, if offered a choice between them and (say) the right to vote or to be a stockbroker, might reasonably choose the former. On any account, it is demonstrably unfair that people (not just women) who are beautiful or handsome, intelligent, popular, talented, and rich should *also* be given other goods—if, that is, we are concerned with justice or if we are concerned with 'equality' *in general* rather than just equality in a particular area.

In the same sort of way we allow the principle of compensation. There is not much money in being a university don, but the work is congenial and there are long holidays. Waiters may sometimes be badly paid but make up on 'perks' of various kinds. Girls commonly prefer jobs where there is a good chance of 'travel' or 'meeting people', which might be seen as advantages, even if the pay is bad. Many men (I am one) may resent the hard work and initiative involved in those sexual circles where it is deemed "up to the man" to take the first step and make most of the moves in courtship; but one might be prepared to put up with this for the sake of sometimes, at least, getting girls who repay one in another coin. Alternatively, one might prefer a different system, a regime of greater 'equality' (which means here, less role differentiation) whereby both parties shared the bills and the work and the sexual initiative. All this, in a very real sense, is a matter of taste.

Justice, in this respect, could only be done if all the contracting parties were reasonably clear about what they wanted or valued (whether by way of power or any other good) and allocated different weights or points to these different things. To anyone who has ever tried it, this becomes immensely complex in at least two ways. First and most obviously, the variety of goods is extremely wide (this is, perhaps, one reason why people tend to concentrate unduly on rather obvious and easily measurable ones, such as money or votes). Suppose I ask the reader to take 1,000 points, consider the categories of goods in their relations with the opposite sex, and assign a number of points to each category in such a way that, if a member of the opposite sex did the same and the results were consolidated, justice would be done. Is that easy? What categories would one use? Money, yes: taking turns to say what we shall do on our nights out, yes, possibly; doing the cooking: doing the washing up ("Yes, but I do the drying": "Ah, but drying is much nicer and easier"); playing with the children—how many points here? What about categories such as not looking erotically at other blondes, or talking too much, or not being at home enough? This shades into the second reason, which is that goods so often depend on the context. Many people (again, I am one) are prepared to overlook, or forgive, or anyway not to want to assign minus points to quite a lot of things, provided they are done *con amore* or if the person apologizes afterward or somehow makes me feel in some very general way, difficult to specify, that my will counts. How can one assign points to goods that slide about like floating island?

Well, one can try and no doubt should try. But if someone raises a complaint about not getting his (her) fair share, that complaint cannot be fairly raised just by itself: the compartments are not watertight. So far as sexual issues are concerned, the crucial question is whether there is any *difference* between the kinds of goods that men and women would, if they were clearheaded about themselves (and not bewitched by too-specific ideas about power and influence), give points to; and, if so, what the difference is. This brings us back full circle to a chapter that appeared earlier, (Chapter 8). I have no more to say here.

11

FEMINIST STRATEGIES

I want to raise, and if possible to answer, some questions about the appropriateness—both practical and moral—of strategies employed by those who may loosely be called "feminists." This is a hopelessly vague description; it is of some significance that even this description could not be used unless there was something like a political or social *group*, if not an organization, to be identified. But it is vaguer than 'suffragettes', which refers specifically to a group with a particular platform, namely, "votes for women." So I must apologize in advance if I am unjust to some who would like to call themselves 'feminists', yet to whose views and behavior little or none of the following applies

We may consider first the 'moral' appropriateness of certain strategies, for here the position is, in my judgment, tolerably clear. It follows, indeed, from some points made in Chapter 9, though with some complications, about the principle (as Mill would put it) of noninterference. In order to justify not only force but the use of nonrational methods—browbeating, blackmail, interference, and various kinds of pressure—applied to other people, we have to be sure that these people are significantly damaging the interests of others. Consequently, any feminist strategies that employ such methods have to show this or be penalized as infringing upon other people's liberty to pursue their own options and interests. Naturally, this does not apply uniquely to feminists: it applies to any group or individual who may use some strategy in the service of an ideal or even of his own selfish interests.

It is important to be clear in advance that we have to interpret this principle fairly strictly and disallow what may appear to be even minor or questionable cases of its infringement in two ways. First, to a person of some sensitivity the wearing of certain colors (even, I suppose, certain skin colors) might be regarded as "offensive" or "damaging to his interests"; but we would not think it right that he should exert nonrational pressure designed to stop people wearing (say) pink dresses or to make them paint themselves white if they were black (or vice versa). We feel that 'damage' is being construed too liberally: he should not be so sensitive, or he should put up with it, or he should look the other way. Of course, there are borderline cases: if someone builds a tall house right next to mine, shutting off the sun, and plays loud music at all times of the day and night, the concept of damage or harm has more of a foothold. We feel this because we feel that almost any normal person could hardly *avoid* seeing this as at least interference, if not harm, whereas we feel that the sensitive aesthete just has some sort of ideal about dress or color, to which he is indeed entitled but which he must not impose on others. Second, a person who had not grasped the point of the principle, and who was overenthusiastic about his ideal, might not go so far as to employ force—violence or imprisonment—on others, but we should not think much of him if, for instance, he never gave them a job, or refused to drink with them, or even if (because of his ideal) he displayed a general coldness or hostility toward them. The point of the principle is not just to avoid civil war but to prevent us from behaving in a "pressurizing" or nonfraternal way toward other men in the hope that, thus inhibited, we may prefer to engage in amicable discussion and interchange instead.

We see, then, that we have to be fairly strict about the concept of "harm" and about the concept of "nonrational methods" or "interference" (Mill's preferred word). Behind all this lies a crucial point—that we must, both in principle and in practice, distinguish sharply between *agreed* forms of damage or harm or offense, about which (we hope) there will be laws and other forms of rules, and various ideals, not necessarily shared by everyone in our society, about which people may indeed feel entirely certain and which (by legitimate methods) they may wish to spend much time and energy promoting, but which are not agreed and institutionalized. We distrust the sensitive aesthete or the person who claims that blacks are 'offensive' just by being visible, because we feel that they are not distinguishing between genuine damage or harm inevitably done to them (and that would be done however tolerant and sane they were) and their insistence that their particular ideals, prescriptions, or preferences prevail. This distinction is crucial. not only in point of reason but to anything that might be called a civilized (let alone a liberal) society.

We have now first to ask whether any feminist strategies use nonrational methods. It is tolerably clear, without going into empirical detail, that they do. There is nothing uniquely antifeminist in this: nearly all groups and individuals do it to some extent, as we are all weak mortals. But (for instance) disrupting beauty competitions, demonstrating in such a way as to be a nuisance to other people, or even (as mentioned above) treating those of opposite opinions with coldness or contempt plainly come within the scope of the principle. The only justification this would have is if it could be shown that those on whom such strategies were employed were, in fact, damaging other people's interests—namely, women's—and that these strategies were necessary to avoid or rectify this damage. So we have now to ask whether this is so: whether, to put it briefly, women are driven to these strategies in order to get their rights.

All this may seem rather long-winded, but there is some need for caution. Answering the question adequately depends on getting a clearer view of what *kinds* of things we are entitled to kick up a fuss about and what kind of fuss we are entitled to kick up. There appear to be three rough categories here:

1. In some cases I might not have any, or enough, power *as a negotiator*—that is, as someone who ought (as, before any specific deals are done, every person ought: see Chapter 9) to have an equal voice in deciding on the rules of the game. Disenfranchised women, or slaves, or philosophers might object to not having the vote on these grounds, irrespective of what *other* powers, rights, or treatment they enjoyed or endured. The objection is simply that they have no say in what these powers, rights, or kinds of treatment are to be.

2. In other cases the *treatment* I get under a particular regime may damage my interests: if women, slaves, and philosophers are beaten up by husbands, slave owners, or university bureaucrats, they are, in a clear sense, harmed or damaged. If they have freely contracted for regimes in which this happens, they cannot complain on grounds of justice; but if they have not, the damage highlights, as it were, or gives a concrete demonstration of what harm is done by the imposition of regimes on unwilling or noncontracting people.

3. In other cases, again, I may have some *ideal* (ideology, set of values, particular picture of how things should be) that the regime does not adequately realize. I might think, for instance, that women should be treated more like men, or more like children; that slaves or serfs would be happier if they participated more, of if they participated less, in day-to-day decision making; or that philosophers should be seen as much more, or much less, important to society than they are now seen.

The practical difficulty, of course, is that what we take to be "unjust" or "oppressive" regimes usually offend us in all three ways: consequently, we have a naively monistic idea of 'oppression' and 'liberation' that leads us to view, and react to, what goes on in particular societies in a monolithic sort of style. It is also possible to see why so many revolutionary or liberationist groups tend to base their thinking on some kind of ideal or ideology rather than on less esoteric principles of justice. For it will seem to them—often quite rightly—that what *causes* the injustice in cases (1.) and (2.) is some kind of social ideology—'capitalism' or 'male chauvinism'—that obliterates both simple negotiating equality and simple justice of treatment. So they are then tempted to *replace* that ideology with another (Marxism, feminism). In just such a way, I suppose, the ideology that led most of the classical Greeks to view women and slaves (though not, fortunately, philosophers) as in some general way 'inferior' was replaced, or is being replaced, by what one might be tempted to call the North American ideology, which regards everyone as in some general way "equal."

Consequently, and understandably, those who want change in such matters are not content to stick with (1.) and (2.): they also see their task as ideological, propagandizing, or—to use a kinder word—*educational*. It is not enough to free the serfs and (thus) ensure that they do not suffer from the knout: they must also come to see the wickedness and false consciousness of capitalist society, the truth of Marxist theories of history, and so forth. So with (some) feminists, it is not enough to have the vote or to receive just treatment in getting jobs, or in trials for rape, or in being paid for housework: they also want men to see women "in the right way." This (*per se* laudable) desire is all the more tempting in that there is, in a clear if somewhat overalluring sense, such a thing as "doing justice to" other people that goes beyond such things—such a thing as seeing them for what they really are, respecting them as persons, or not imposing stereotypes on them.

But (as Mill very clearly saw) the proper vehicle for negotiating *this* kind of business is education and rational discussion. I stress 'education', not indoctrination or propaganda, because many revolutionaries (and, of course, many conservatives) make no clear distinction—the distinction, as we should know by now, partly, at least, consisting of the one we have already made between nonpressurizing and pressurizing methods. The fact is, as we know quite well when we stop to think, that we do *not* want to subscribe to a rule in virtue of which we can all impose our ideals and ideologies—our pictures of what it is to 'do justice to' various people and problems—on each other without restraint. This is why we have to distinguish between interfering with somebody—a neo-Nazi, for instance—who is simply propounding his views, however absurd in our opinion, and interfering with somebody who actually lynches blacks or beats up Pakistanis. It is tempting to blur the distinction, because we feel that words and ideologies lead to deeds; nevertheless, we are right to hold our fire and wait for the deeds, just as we are right not to penalize drunkenness *per se*, but only to penalize it when the drunkard is a manifest danger (when driving, for instance). Without this distinction most of the specific freedoms—including free speech—beloved by liberal societies would rapidly vanish.

Nor is it unimportant to note that there are logical (not only empirical) impossibilities in doing *total* justice, indeed, in doing anything like justice, to other people in this sense. It takes at least a lifetime even to begin to do justice to even one woman. Inevitably—and the point is independent of what particular stereotypes or pictures one has of women—since one does not know all about her, certain features will be stressed, or be "salient," at the expense of others. Nor should we take 'at the expense of' too seriously—it is to say no more than that one may notice certain things and not certain other things about, say, a Shakespeare play not only on first reading but on any subsequent reading. One notices, perhaps, the plot or certain beautiful lines of verse 'at the expense' of the characterization or certain other lines. Would it even *mean* anything to say that one had done 'complete justice' to the play?

There are two standard feminist reactions here, both (again) understandable but ultimately unsatisfactory. The first is to suggest that, unlike the Shakespeare case, A ought to see B in the way that B *wants* to be seen (I suppose Shakespeare might be said to have an interest in how we see his plays: but he is dead). The trouble here is that, if we are now talking about the merits of particular ideals as such (irrespective of who entertains them), there is no particular reason to believe that the way in which B wants to be seen actually represents the right ideal: B, for instance, may be a male-dominated woman in a state of 'false consciousness' and A, a truly liberated man (assuming they do exist) who sees her as fully equal. Feminist sympathies would then, I imagine, be with A; but then the criterion of how B wants to be seen is useless. We can jump the other way and say that the criterion of how B wants to be seen should be preserved, irrespective of whether B has the right ideal, although now we have jumped back from the promotion of a particular ideology into the area of general equality and justice. This represents the bind in which all overenthusiastic revolutionaries are caught: Marxists have the same difficulty with the working classes who do not (it may seem) actually want the revolution to happen.

The second reaction, somewhat more plausible, is to insist on a much higher standard of at least *trying* to see people 'for what they really are'. Here the Shakespeare case may be preserved, since we might think it morally disreputable, or at least rather slack, not to do our best to 'appreciate' the play for what it was really worth. This brings in the idea of "using people," discussed earlier.[1] We seem obliged to say that there is nothing positively *wrong* either in seeing people only in certain aspects (as pretty, or good tennis partners, or philosophers) or in restricting the kind of business we do with them to those aspects (kissing, playing tennis, doing philosophy). We might say, at most, that it was rather a *pity* that someone saw *Hamlet* only as a blood-and-thunder thriller; we would, no doubt, encourage people to get as much as they could out of various worthwhile objects and out of each other. But the facts are that there is a limit (again, a logical as well as an empirical limit) to how much time and effort one can put into this.

To put some of this in a more practical way: there are various things that are or might be true about me that, if only by some stretch of a febrile imagination, might be thought to represent various *species boni* or "standard interests." Suppose I have a first-class degree from Oxford; or I might be physically appealing, or able to do the *Times* crossword, or good at table tennis. Now, suppose various women keep coming to me and (apparently) wanting to talk about Oxford philosophy or wanting me to help them with the crossword and that few, if any, throw their arms round me and say, "You handsome erotic brute, you!" If I had too much of this, I should certainly be tempted to say, "It is all most depressing, they only want me for my brains, really the stereotypes women have."; and certainly in any long-sustained relationship, I should hope that they would— and perhaps would actually try to persuade them to—see me as more than a crossword expert or someone who has "the right sort of degree" or as more than any of the other things that I myself take for granted and that I feel are already more than adequately catered for. Actually, I should probably find that *persuasion* was not a very good weapon: people see one in the way they want to and are likely to extend their range or sophisticate their perceptions of others only by a general increase of trust and experience, not to say love. My attitude basically ought to be, I take it, something like, "Well, it is nice that they like me for PQR—at least that is something, and we can share that together; and perhaps in time they will come to see that I am also XYZ and that this represents something that can also be shared." Anything like resentment or coldness or hostility toward them because they did not appreciate *all* my features, or because they singled out ones that I *myself* did not particularly value, would be clearly unreasonable: the former, because it is logically absurd and the latter, because (among other reasons) what they valued about me might well be more important than what I valued.

One of the points made *en passant* in the course of this example may shed some light on the prudential, rather than the moral, aspects of feminist strategies. I have granted that there is nothing wrong, and plainly there is a good deal right, in wanting people to be more *educated* (reasonable, understanding, et cetera) in this whole area, as opposed to pressurizing them in various ways so as to promote a particular ideal. Now, if *this* is the enterprise—if, whether feminism may be classified as a political movement, it will at least be a political movement that has *education* as its goal—there are some things we may be able to say. In particular, we may be able to say something (1) about what particular educational goods or kinds of learning we are out to promote and (2) about what the necessary preconditions for that kind of learning are. Thus, in the example, if I take seriously the job of educating my girl friends, what do I have to attend to?

Perhaps the first thing to do here is to enter the same moral *caveat*. There is, as I am sure some feminist readers will have been quick to note, something slightly arrogant in the idea of educating people who are or might be one's friends—certainly in the much more suspicious idea of thinking that this education will necessarily consist of making sure that they have *my* views on how they ought to see me as a man or as a person. There are two points here. First, education is tied to the notion of some kind of *impersonal* truth or understanding—I have, as it were, not *authority* in the matter of how they should come to see me; or, if I were to have any, it could only be because I could be seen, in some general way, as possessing more psychological insight, philosophical clarity, or scientific understanding of male-female differences, or something of that kind. Second, even if one established such authority, that in itself would still not allow us to *impose* (insofar as one can successfully impose) the task of education on other people who do not want to be educated. If I were to say to my women students, "Yes, I will eventually relate to you and do various kinds of business with you, but you are in such a state of false consciousness that I insist that you undergo a three-year course, designed by myself, entitled 'The Proper Attitude to Adopt to the Male Sex,'" this would rightly be regarded as not far short of tyranny.

We may, of course, legitimately hope that opportunities for mutual education will arise naturally in the course of relationships and that individuals will be inspired to learn on their own by reading the relevant literature, searching their hearts, getting clear about the relevant concepts, and so forth. But this is different: if feminists are out to educate, they cannot use force or pressure and justify it in the name of education. For, again, education represents *one* ideal that, at least in part, a person may (reasonably or unreasonably) reject. It would be quite in order for a woman to say, "For goodness' sake, let's stop *educating each other and just enjoy each other.*"

This *caveat* entered ([1] above), we might fairly say that feminists are out to promote and encourage (not, now, by illegitimate pressure) certain kinds of learning and understanding. The difficulty is to see how this can effectively be done under some such heading as 'a proper understanding of women' or 'sexism'. Some of the difficulties here I have commented on at greater length elsewhere. But, very briefly, it seems that all or most of the concepts, principles, and kinds of understanding that rational feminists want people to grasp are too *general* to go under those headings. The same point applies to black studies, Oxford-don studies, pygmy studies, and other such; one has the strong suspicion that the criteria used to demarcate such alledgedly educational groups are not educational but political. Thus, among the contents of such education would be, presumably, a better understanding of what counts as a relevant difference (what, if anything, is the force of "Because he is black," "Because she is a woman," et cetera), a proper grasp of what a person is and what it is to respect persons, and the various highly general points about equality, sex, love, justice, and so on that we have looked at in this book. Indeed, it could really be only on grounds of public relations or motivation that the book should have the title it does: from a strictly intellectual viewpoint, it is a work of *philosophy*, irrespective of what it is *about*.

This is, of course, somewhat too harsh, since it might fairly be argued that, though the goals are to educate people (which means giving them a better grasp of particular concepts and general principles), (a) we can legitimately cash in on the fact that many people might be *motivated* to learn, or at least are more like-ly actually to turn up, because of their political or idiosyncratic interests (in being a woman, or an Oxford don, or black, or a pygmy, or whatever): and (b) that *some* of what they learn is specific to feminist interests—for instance, the history of women, the sociology of women, I suppose even the biology of wo-men. That this last item sounds odd, however, is surely due to the fact that in-sofar as we are genuinely concerned with education, and *not* with the advance-ment of some political cause, we usually classify things under the appropriate subjects of disciplines: feminine biology comes under biology, not under wo-men's studies. My guess is that, if we entirely forswear the political, we should not have the latter classification at all, or not much.

What will actually *induce* people to learn is ([2] above), in large part, an empirical question. It is entirely possible that by making demonstrations, holding up the traffic, buttonholing people, or knocking on their doors with feminist literature—assuming, which is not always clear, that there is social a-greement that legitimizes these methods as nonpressurizing—education will be promoted, although, again, it seems better to fit the idea of advancing some cause or trying to get one's rights, which throws us back to moral rather than prudential considerations. I doubt, however, whether a full discussion would turn out to be solely, or even primarily, empirical, as I shall try briefly to show. For a great deal would depend on what *particular* kinds of learning were thought by feminists to be important; from this the kinds of methods or preconditions would, in large part, follow (as indeed, despite "learning theorists" and other kinds of psychologists, is true for education and learning in general).

Thus, suppose (as I myself believe) that one of the most basic difficulties (perhaps the most basic) is that men—and, no doubt, women—have certain psychological vested interests that cause them to see the opposite sex in certain ways (even, perhaps, to describe it as "opposite"). Let us say, for instance, that men are rather frightened of women and uncertain about their mysterious pow-ers; so that, as a kind of defense or screening system, they tend to see them of-ten as conquerable objects, or pretty little things, or whatever. Now, as any com-petent psychiatrist knows, learning of this kind requires a great deal of trust and security before it can seriously proceed at all: it is entirely useless, and may be worse than useless, to beat the person about the ears with the intention of mak-ing him change his attitude—whatever may appear to happen on the surface, the defenses are simply reinforced. When we are incensed about something (even about ignorance), there is a standing temptation to do something that will make people "sit up and think." Well, no doubt they sit up, and no doubt they react, and they may even think: but changing an attitude is much more than this. At-titudes have, as it were, a case history that nearly always involves some kind of *fear*—without diminishing this, nothing of much significance happens.

It depends on what we want. If feminists want—what for their *political* objectives may be entirely proper—something like a social tradition in which women are, in some broad sense, accepted as equals, work side by side with men, are allowed to do any job, and so forth, this is one thing. This is rather like saying that we want science, rather than astrology or witchcraft, to flourish in a society: we want it to be, as it were, institutionalized and socially visible. But so to educate people that they come to have a genuinely scientific *attitude*, an attitude that they will hang on to despite temptations to the contrary, is something else. Here institutionalization is extremely fragile, as the corruption of science in Nazi Germany and other such cases abundantly show or, indeed, as the modern tendency to go in for astrology and various other nonscientific fantasies shows. There is, then, at least a question about how far—in principle, and ultimately in point of logic—what might be called 'social' or 'administrative', or even 'political' moves can effectively *educate*. They can, of course, help to keep the ring for, or enable preconditions to be established for, education: but, in most important matters, that may be all. People are not educated out of prejudice *simply* by being forced to mix with other classes or colors or creeds: we recognize this because we recognize that there is a conceptual misfit between what is implied by 'prejudice' and what is implied by these 'social' methods.

Many liberationist and revolutionary groups seem to take the view (sometimes even without prior reflection or argument) that most or all educational failure is due to "society." Had people not been "socially conditioned," or if we had a society that removed this misplaced conditioning, it is thought, people would grow up to have just views of the opposite sex, blacks, Oxford dons, and other people in general. This suggests an extremely naive or monistic view of the multiplicity of causes that generate things such as prejudice and misperception: it would be very odd if *some* of the causes were not "social" but, for instance, had more to do with the child's early years (irrespective of what sort of parents he has) and the unconscious mind. Indeed, there are some necessary truths here, not just empirical facts, on which we have commented earlier (see Chapters 3, 6, and 8). But even if this were not so, only an extreme Rousseauesque or Wordsworthian view of human nature—the uncorrupted, unalienated, naturally good and virtuous child—would enable the founders of a new society to dispense with the task of considering just how its members are to *learn* to see people in the right way.

In considering this, it is tolerably clear that the founders will need more than "social conditioning": they will require that the members, as children, come to grasp certain concepts and principles in the light of which they form the appropriate attitudes and behave in appropriate ways. To this, there is bound (even in the ideal society) to be strong resistance, even if only the resistance of one who finds thinking hard and clarity difficult to attain: laziness, perhaps, or original sin, or the egocentrism natural to all men, or whatever we may want to say—but not just 'social conditioning'. I am tempted to say that, with feminism as with any serious problem, anyone who thinks that the right answers are *obvious*, or that it is *easy* to obtain a just view, or that we can be so *certain* of our views that we can expend our time and energy on furthering a partisan set of be-liefs, has hardly even started.

NOTES

1. John Wilson, "Education and Identity, " in *Fantasy and Common Sense in Education* (Oxford: Martin Robertson, 1979).

12

ABORTION

The topic of abortion is included in Part II because it has no very direct conceptual connection with what is "sexual" in the sense of the word *erotic* that we have been concerned with in Part I and because it has at least this much connection with feminism—that a good deal of the problem seems to be about *whose* interests are at stake (and what those interests consist of): if not, as most feminists would claim, just the mother's, then whose else's?

In a well-known article (to which, for reasons of space, I cannot give the word-by-word attention it deserves) R. M. Hare claims, in effect, that abortion can be dealt with by his theory of universal prescription, or the 'Golden Rule', on the grounds that embryos are persons-to-be, who can (in all relevant senses) be identified or individuated and that harming a person-to-be's interests in in effect like harming an existing person's interests (as, for instance, one can harm the interests of future generations by present pollution).[1] There seems to be something badly wrong with this, which may be intuitively expressed by saying, "But persons-to-be are not people." Perhaps in trying to make this more precise we may come to see more clearly what *kind* of problem, at least, abortion presents.

Part of the oddity is that one of the basic moves in this sort of theory involves saying something such as, "How would *you* like it if. . . ?" Whatever the difficulties with this move, it is obviously intelligible if we add things such as, ". . .*your* salary was halved?" or ". . .*your* home was robbed?" "How would *you* like it if *you* had not been born?" is odd, for there is no unborn "you" to like, or choose, or prescribe, or anything else. Given that I exist, I may choose, more or less reasonably, to prolong my life or end it. I may also imagine myself as a soul or person with a chance of being born and as choosing whether to go in for a human life or not—but this is a palpable fiction. There is, anyway, some kind of important difference between questions of the form, (1) "Given that there are or are going to be people, how should we behave in relation to their interests?" and questions of the form, (2) "Shall there be people, or a person—shall we produce some, and if so, how many?" We object to pollution in the present because of its effect on future people, because we know that there will actually *be* future people. Whether there *ought* to be is another matter.

If we make the (to my mind, fatal) move of assuming that embryos are, in effect and for all or most moral purposes, people—because they are —then we place ourselves firmly and consistently in the camp of those who take abortion to be murder. 'Murder' is a term we use for the killing of rational or conscious creatures when this is not legitimated (or thought to be legitimated) by some special set of rules (for example, in time of war). This would enforce the view—which, curiously, Hare does not take—that abortion would always be wrong unless one could show that the interests of other people (perhaps the mother) were even more severely damaged than the person-to-be's interests were damaged by killing him. Since the loss of one's life is normally taken as a pretty severe form of damage, this would be hard to show. It would certainly not be sufficient to say, "Well, this particular pregnancy is unfortunate, it affects my health adversely, and the child may not have much of a life, . . .and I can always have another child under happier circumstances, so the best thing is to abort." Not only insufficient but largely irrelevant, it confuses the question (1) of what to do about an entity who (in this view) as a person-to-be has rights and interests *in the same sense* as a proper person has with the question (2) of whether, and when, to go in for producing another person.

This, I take it, is the point of introducing science fiction-type examples: not with the implication that our moral principles ought always to be framed so as to cover any logically possible cases (rather than those cases that we are actually likely to meet) but in order to pin down *what it is about* embryos that we feel to be important, what sort of *moral status* they have. If someone were to say, as Hare seems to say, that it consists in their *capacity* to become persons (with some additional clause such as "in the normal course of events"), then anything else that comes under that rubric will have the same status. Now we have only to imagine, rather as in Aldous Huxley's *Brave New World*, that children can be produced externally—and "in the normal course of events"—by, for example, passing electric charges through certain chemical combinations in test tubes; what is in the test tubes has the capacity to become a person, and the particular combination in each test tube can (we suppose) be identified and individuated; how do we now feel if somebody upsets the test tube deliberately or refuses to pass the electric charge?

This is not a rhetorical question, triumphantly expecting the answer, "We wouldn't mind at all" and to be followed by, "There you are, it is all just senti-ment, nothing to do with the capacity for life: you are just misled by the contin-gent facts that embryos have certain human characteristics, that they are a form of life, that they are closely associated with the mother's body, and so on." For plainly (though not in Huxley) parents might invest a good deal of feeling in their particular test tube, watching it grow into something recognizably human and being genuinely upset when it was upset. There *is*, indeed, an appropriate at-titude or set of attitudes to be taken toward a variety of objects: we might try a rough classification in terms of (1) life ("respect for life"), (2) human life (the existence of rational creatures), (3) "potential" human life (embryos, whether in wombs or test tubes), and (4) potential human life (which is, in some sense, one's own or uniquely connected with oneself, as it were, one's own *property*).

This classification will certainly not do as it stands (for one thing, the idea of something being uniquely connected with oneself, in [4], applies across other categories and is not a discrete item), but it may help us a bit further forward. To begin with (1): the (popular) idea of "respect for life" certainly has something in it, but what precisely? If we take "life" in accordance with scien-tific criteria, we seem obliged to 'respect' or 'value' not only dogs and cats and embryos, not only wasps and flies and beetles, but also bacilli and viruses. More-over, is it really *life* that is the central notion here? Certainly something is wrong with someone who, devoid of any feeling, simply squashes butterflies or even beetles without reason; but it might be, or partly be, the *same* thing that is wrong with those who slash at beautiful flowers with sticks when walking, or de-face oil paintings, or destroy complex machinery. We ought not, one might say, to destroy *flourishing things* or things that have some value in themselves. Living things are, no doubt, an important subclass of these, perhaps with their own ap-propriate attitudes ("only God can make a tree"), but in any case, so far as abor-tion is concerned, the category is far too wide.

Human life (2), on the other hand, is too narrow to include embryos. When we are think of rights, interests, points of view, options, and so forth—and a great deal of our moral language moves in this dimension—we are thinking of creatures who are rational and conscious in the way that (so far as I know) em-bryos are not: that is, creatures who have language, can report on their own lan-guage using, or have some conceptualization in terms of space and time, cause and effect, right and wrong—in fact, creatures who are *people*. It is of the es-sence to me as a person that I have some body or embodiment, but not *this* body or anything like it: should my brain, mind, or memories be removed and put into a robotic shell, I should still be me. This has nothing, or need not have anything, to do with what we are going to mean by "person": there is a cutoff point, difficult to detect in many practical cases (apes? newborn infants? dogs? dolphins?) but viable in theory, between creatures in one class and creatures in another. Embryos, at least for most of their existence, fall outside the class to which we ascribe points of view, intentions, language, and the rest of the (conceptually interwoven) paraphernalia that make up a rational creature or a person.

With categories (3) and (4) we are on much more uncertain ground, but it is at least the right ground to map out. We might start by saying, very minimally, that it is a *pity*—a cause for regret—if life (or any valuable thing) is destroyed; it is more of a pity (or perhaps a different kind of pity) if (3) it is potentially human life: and if (4) it is potentially a human life that is one's own, or unique to oneself in some way, it is more of a pity still. What we need to get some grip on is the *kind* of pity it is in each case or *why* it is a pity. Is it, for instance, just a matter of regret (that *we* have lost something), or is remorse appropriate (we feel we have done something wrong, that we are *guilty* in some way)? If remorse, what should we feel the guilt *about*, since, other things being equal, there is no *person's* interests that we have harmed?

One apparent way out leads to a cul-de-sac, though an important one: it involves the claim that some things in human life, life as in fact we have it, either are or ought to be nonnegotiable. Thus, it might be said that it either could not, or ought not to, be the case that men and women felt about aborting their own future children in the way that they characteristically felt about, for instance, destroying larvae or frog spawn, or even about drowning kittens. One chooses the words *could not* perhaps for certain basic psychological reasons immune (and perhaps rightly immune) to rational discussions and *ought not* perhaps because any such discussion could do no more—if it could do anything—than to corrupt a practical syllogism essential for any satisfactory human life. Human beings are not infinitely flexible: it just may not be possible to produce a human being with the right sort of feelings and tendencies to act unless there are certain things he could not bring himself to do or could not bring himself to do without feeling stricken by guilt—if we tried to do this, by sophisticating his moral principles so that they allowed him to make exceptions when necessary, we should produce only moral monsters.

This is not *per se* absurd, but the trouble is, in part, that we do not *know* what (if there are any) these nonnegotiable elements are (or should be). In order to find out what they are, we have *first* to consider what we believe to be right, and only *then* consider whether and how we can make our feelings match up to it. After we have done this—if you like, purely intellectual—exercise, we may indeed find some nonnegotiable elements, although we shall also, no doubt, find plenty of features that had been taken as nonnegotiable that, in fact, are simply the results of prejudice, social conditioning, or psychological fantasy. So, although the cul-de-sac is worth noting—for we may partly be stuck with it—we have to retrace our steps.

The peculiarity about embryos is perhaps this: we have some intensity of feeling about aborting them, yet it is not clear (despite our moral protestation) that it is about them *as life*, or even as human life, or as things flourishing, that we have these feelings. Or at least, if we do, it is plausible to argue that the feelings are mere sentiment: the same kind of sentiment as we might feel about killing animals—sentiment that would be absent in societies where animals were necessary for food or where there was no such thing as artificial contraception. This sort of sentiment might be a kind of high-minded luxury, an almost aesthetic delicacy of feeling that might amount to not much more than a desire to keep one's hands clean; we should not be thinking so much of the value ('interests' is a perfectly proper term here, since not only rational creatures have interests) of the entity itself but of our moral style, so to speak. For the fact is—if I am not merely trying to bully the reader—that there is not much to be said in favor of embryos as flourishing entities in their own right: they are, palpably, not like beautiful butterflies that we do not want squashed, or the Mona Lisa that we do not want defaced, or even a delicate and complex piece of machinery that we do not want smashed. What we value—and Hare is, in a way, basically right about this—is their *potentiality*.

It is, again, perhaps a bit suspiciously high-minded to say that we value their potentiality as human beings: there are, after all, plenty of human beings (more than enough, we might think) and plenty more likely to appear in the future. Much more plausible is the connection between the embryo and, as one might rather brutally put it, its *owners*. It is reported that one man tried to prevent his wife's attempted abortion on the grounds that he wanted an heir, that he had a vested interest in the fetus as a kind of property. This, though perhaps (as I have described it, no doubt with some injustice) suggesting a rather narrow-minded or feudal idea about the general purposes of having children, is nevertheless on the right sort of lines. *A fortiori* the mother, if—an important "if", as we shall see—she values the fetus as a future person, even as a child, naturally feels intense regret if she decides to abort it. Regret, not remorse, is surely more appropriate here, if I am right in suggesting that we are basically concerned with *our* interests, or at best with the (future) interests of something *we want* to create rather than with the interests of the embryo *per se*.

If remorse has any sort of foothold, it would not be in any direct way—that is, not in any way that directly connected with the embryo's interests. We might go so far as to say, perhaps, that there is something wrong, or something "missing," with people (perhaps particularly a sexual couple) who regarded the possibility of children and the actuality of pregnancy as merely boring or tiresome: not that they (in any direct action-guiding sense) *ought* to want children and decide to have them but rather that children represent a standard human interest that, when they are brought up against it (by the pregnancy), they ought at least to recognize and have some kind of feelings about. Thus, one might suddenly find oneself landed with a dog, for example, although one might well rightly decide to get rid of it, since one's life was too full of other standard interests to have space for it, nevertheless, there would be something wrong if one simply "got rid of it" in the same way as one would get rid of bits of dust or dirt: not because of the *dog's* interests but because one would recognize that the dog represented something in which human beings could—and in principle, if time allows, should—be interested. A better parallel might be if, for instance, having no interest in agriculture or gardening, I suddenly find that my terrain is impregnated with the seeds of some remarkable plant or vegetable: the seeds have begun to grow and keen gardeners come and say how lucky I am. I need not be concerned with the plant's interests, but if I uproot them because I do not want the bother of tending them when full-grown, I recognize that I am not doing justice to a worthwhile enterprise. There can be a sort of remorse here, not so much about what one does as about what one is: "I wish I were the sort of person who liked plants and gardens," perhaps coupled with, "Maybe if I really tried and bought some books about it, I could get to like it and be a better person in this respect." One can have remorse, not just regret, about ideals, because ideals are not just a matter of prudence.

If this is on the right lines, then it appears that embryos should be regarded as a kind of property: a very special kind, indeed, meriting certain attitudes and not others—but property, inasmuch as decisions about abortion must be left to the owners. The question remains, of course, who the owners actually are and what respective rights they have but the problem is at least manageable in principle if not in practice. As with most problems in that *genre*, almost everything seems to depend on good communication—that is, on those parties responsible for the situation setting up a clear and detailed contract in the first place, a contract that does justice to the options of each (see Chapter 9). Thus, if the wife agrees to provide an heir, even if the pregnancy is unpleasant, though not if it positively threatens her life, in return for husbandly care—and so on, with clauses and provisos spelled out—well, then *that* is the agreement, however "servile" or "unliberated" some may take it to be. Or if the woman wishes to adopt a much more independent attitude, whereby she takes full responsibility for the pregnancy and the child, giving the husband clearly to understand that he has no obligations, well, then *that* is the agreement.

Questions about the *control* of abortion are, thus, in a clear sense, political questions, for the answers to which we go back to the usual principles of justice and contract theory. This is to say that, embryos being a form of property, we do right if we allocate decisions about whether it is right or wrong to abort to particular parties, not to the State or to some national 'moral consensus'. In cases where the contract between the two parties is not clearly spelled out, the parties themselves should settle the matter on the same principles of justice, roughly (as we say in Chapter 9) on the grounds of what they *would* have contracted for if asked, or on some version of Hare's theory of universal prescription. In practice, it usually turns out to be right to let the mother decide, since it is (usually) her interests that are most at stake. The important thing is to get the contracts clear in the first place.

There is, however, an extra twist to this in the case of abortion, again connected with the crucial fact that it is the future of the fetus in which we are most interested. For if embryos are not (in the required sense) people, children certainly are: and it is not at all clear that the decision to have a child can be entrusted unilaterally to the parents, since we are now talking not just about property but about the interests of people. There are two obvious worries here. First, we may be thinking about the population problem and want to introduce some form of rationing: the difficulties here are mainly those mentioned earlier, that of producing sufficiently good communication to enable clear and just contracts to be made. I will say no more than that I should guess that, *if* such communication were ensured (as why, in principle, should it not be?), almost everyone would come to agree on some form of rationing and that those who feel most deeply concerned about the population problem would do best to expend their energies on improving communication in this sense. Second, however, it is not at all clear that any couple who feels like having a child can be trusted to give him adequate care: this calls for some collective decision, since the child's interests are at stake—in many cases, it might have been better to abort the embryo in the first place.

I am not sure how much of a strictly philosophical nature there is to be said about this. What is to count as "adequate care" is, of course, disputable and also elusive: love seems to be as important as attention to health or even to food, and the obvious danger in laying down criteria is that the criteria tend to be behavioristic and bureaucratic, allowing the important elements to slip through the meshes of regulations. But it might be at least plausible to suggest that potential parents be required to show some evidence of good faith: for instance, that they have lived together in reasonable amity for a certain length of time (so that the child has a fair chance of a stable home) and that they have actually *thought* about the desirability of having a child. One is hesitant in making even such apparently obvious suggestions as these, for fear that the stable home will be rendered unstable by the invasion of official agents trying (no doubt from the best of motives) to impose *their* (or the general public's) picture of "a happy home" on the parents, without rational justification. But there seems, in my view of the immense amount of real damage to real children (never mind embryos) caused by parental incompetence, vice, mental illness, or some other evil, to be a strong case for at least making potential parents measure up to *some* set of criteria designed to make them appreciate that children, at least, are not property but people in their own right. The actual practice of abortion would, I think, be (rightly) affected as much by this as by any other points to be made.

NOTES

1. R. M. Hare, "Abortion and the Golden Rule," in *Philosophy and Sex*, ed. Robert Baker and Frederick Elliston (Buffalo, N.Y.: Prometheus Books, 1975).

POSTSCRIPT: SEX AND EDUCATION

I append this postscript not just because education happens to be my job but for the connected reasons that (1) it is, in an important sense, everyone's job: 'educational' may describe a mode or aspect of human relationships—we educate each other; (2) sex education is unlikely to be much good unless based on a proper understanding of the relevant concepts, to which I have tried to contribute in this book; and (3) there is ultimately not much point in getting clear about the concepts unless this clarity is put to educational use. The main difficulties, I think, lie in the *interface* between philosophy and educational practice: and I attempt here only to give some idea of the problems that may be found there.

One point, perhaps fairly obvious, is that we need to keep a firm grasp of what must be the *core* of anything properly to be called sex education. If, as might be said by someone who relied on the "biological" sense of 'sex' and 'sexuality', scientific and practical knowledge about the reproductive organs, contraception, et cetera were considered central, there might be little or no case for having a special category called 'sex education' at all—or, at best, a case based only on purely practical considerations (as we might want 'driver education' or 'house-buying and mortgage-getting education'). For all or most of this would naturally be taught under the appropriate scientific heading—biology, or physiology, or whatever—just as, if we wanted for some reason to teach the history of sexual behavior, this would come most naturally under the general heading of history. I am not saying that the basic and important biological facts and techniques should not, if necessary, be taught: often it will be necessary. But this is not enough and not central—indeed, not even strictly relevant—to sexuality in the sense of eroticism.

For much the same sort of reasons, the idea of regarding sex education as centrally a matter of *skills* or *techniques* seems equally wrong. No one denies that there is such a thing as being a skillful lover or mistress or that it is useful to be aware of certain sexual techniques: it might even be said, in a somewhat extended sense of 'skill', that there were various "social skills" useful for boys and girls to learn for purposes of courtship or ordinary human interaction: "How to Behave on Your First Date," and that sort of thing. But—quite apart from the dangers of inducing a kind of blind conformity—none of this seems central to *sexuality*: we are talking of things that may be useful *in the service of sexuality* only, which is why we call them "skills" or "techniques." This remains true even if we consider the possibility of placing boys and girls, at an appropriate age, in the hands of erotic experts (rather as scions of the English aristocracy were placed in the hands of Parisian ladies who taught them how to behave in bed). Not that this might not be very helpful and, indeed, seems plainly to be advocated: at least it impinges on the central area of sexuality, which (as we have seen) has something to do with our attitude toward our own bodies, and those of other people, as erotic objects. Much may be learned thus, and the learning would go far beyond what is covered by the term 'skill': no doubt students would come to understand much more about how they felt erotically, the kind of desires and fears they had. The trouble is, of course, that it is a contrived situation: the emotions on both sides are given or blanked out because of prior stipulations. Yet it is, surely, just those emotions that cause a good deal of the trouble. We want to know how to feel about the people we meet under normal circumstances, not just about Parisian demimondaines. (Readers of Dorothy Sayers will remember that the aristocratic hero, Wimsey, passed the demimondaine test with flying colors but then lost his heart totally for some years to a quite unsuitable girl "of gossamer and moonshine.")

This represents a general danger, the danger of the contrived, and might tempt one to say that sex education if billed as a special item on the program, is really a nonstarter. Another part of the danger is that, insofar as we deal with any more than biological fact, there is the likelihood—as things are in all or almost all societies and schools, perhaps the inevitability—that all we shall succeed in doing is to impose or encourage a certain kind of sexual ideal. Some social groups put pressure on the individual to be, in the old-fashioned sense, chaste or others to be promiscuous; others, again, demand a kind of sexual athleticism, inducing guilt or shame in those that fail in the pentathlon; yet others expect children to grow up with a high degree of sensitivity to what is "decent" or "unfitting." Certainly, unless and until teachers in schools and elsewhere have a clear understanding of what a rational kind of sex education would look like and have the powers actually to carry it out (in the teeth of parents, "society," and other pressure groups), educators are unlikely to be able to do much except reinforce one or another of these models. And, again, if all we do is to make the usual moral points about respect for persons, treating others as equals, and so on, we have produced nothing specific to *sexuality*.

The other difficulty, analyzed in Chapter 3, is that there is inevitably something 'special' or 'private' about sexuality; any attempt to treat sex education breezily, as if it were a kind of cross between hygiene and hockey, must fail since it takes sex to be something other than it is. (This is one of the points at which 'degraded' may be an appropriate term.) It is maddening when pupils giggle and whisper about sex, in class or out of it, but there is, in a real sense, something for them to giggle and whisper about. We may reasonably say that we want pupils to grasp that sex is something "perfectly normal," "natural," "nothing to be ashamed of," and so on, but we cannot reasonably say that we want them to treat it like eating or excretion. If we try, the pupils will know better.

The only hope—but it is enough—lies in the emotions: and I take sex education, in any reputable sense, to be a branch of the education of the emotions. There are, as we saw in Chapter 3, reasons why some emotions will necessarily enter into sexuality, and it is, in fact, just these that cause young people the most trouble and anxiety. Among these are such things as fear of rejection, vulnerability, the desire of conquest, loneliness, love and affection, tenderness, aggression, and many others together with the more obvious defense mechanisms that allow us to deny them to ourselves and to others—male *machismo*, female prudishness, an assumed disinterest in eroticism, an overvaluation of it, and so on. Granted that, even in these days of literacy and the mass media, boys and girls will still be ignorant and worried about biological facts, nevertheless, my guess is that most of their worries exist precisely in the area where adults keep their worries—that is, the area of the emotions.

It may still be said: "But if there are no specifically *sexual* emotions, how can this sort of education stand as a category in its own right? Should we not simply run courses and lay on learning experiences in the general area of the emotions, and that would take care of sexuality—just as it would take care of other practical areas, such as war or friendship or the family?" There is some force in this from the strictly philosophical viewpoint (if this is the right way to put it); yet, there is clearly a sense, as we have seen, in which sexuality is more fundamental, and less contingent, to human nature than those other areas. For that reason alone it deserves special attention—though still under the general heading of "educating the emotions": I am not arguing for one or another set of practical details, such as whether to have time-tabled periods or whether to use the *title* "sex education." Apart from the (quite important) practical fact that sex is, like it or not, already a separate category in pupils' minds and that they are worried about it, I take there to be two arguments in favor of a special category. First, as Freud rightly saw, sexuality is of such basic importance that it serves as a kind of paradigm or model case, also as some kind of indicator, for a person's emotional psychic state. Second, not *all* emotions tend to enter into sexuality, though a good many may, so that there is a reasonable hope of narrowing the field in a way practical enough to justify a category. Without a fully worked out list of all the emotions, together with their targets or objects, characteristic beliefs, and so on—a task of crucial importance that yet remains to be done—it is very hard to say which emotions will play a part and which will not; but we have, perhaps, enough experience or intuition to know what is most likely here.

It should not need to be said that education in this area will extend its range from the 'academic'—for instance, a proper conceptual understanding—to the "practical." What is important, as I have pointed out elsewhere,[1] is the carer: I mean (as in all or most education), the task of getting the pupils to move from the understanding of general concepts and principles to practical cases in their own experience and back again. It is no good simply understanding the principles or simply having the experiences: each needs to be monitored in the light of the other, and with the help of someone with insight and experience. Somewhere in between these poles, presumably, will come methods such as role playing, the use of literature, simulation situations, films, impromptu drama, and so forth. All this has been discussed at length in the literature, and I need not go into it here.

One point, however, is crucial. Because of the fundamental nature of sex, there is likely to be more resistance to the task of learning here than in other areas—even in other areas of the education of the emotions. So far as education is concerned, the place for 'love' is not as a kind of ideal that, in a high-minded but misguided way, we try to persuade pupils to glue onto their natural eroticism—this is up to them—but in the educator's own mind or heart. Unless he has the kind of benevolent detachment and concern that generates enough trust for the pupils to let their psychic hair down, not much of any real value can be done: for unless they own up to their emotions, there is no real material to work with—we can talk about impersonal cases till doomsday (and something can be gained by that), but something much more important happens if and when they learn to admit their own feelings to themselves and to others. Naturally, this cannot be forced, as any sensible person knows, although it can be powerfully encouraged by the right sort of background conditions, proper setting of the stage, and even by habit and practice. The teacher has obvious devices in his armory (such as being the first to "own up" or show himself human). Since pupils and teachers vary, the best thing would be to leave it up to the teachers themselves.

All this raises a general question that applies to moral education as a whole, although its force is perhaps particularly obvious here. Most of the practical problems and discussions about sexuality in relation to education—about the "suitability" of certain literature or TV programs, what constitutes the "proper" relationships between teacher and pupils, and so on—usually and unsurprisingly fail to distinguish between *educational* goods in this area and other goods. It will not, I take it, be disputed that educational goods must at least be those acquired by *learning*. We should naturally expect anything called *sex education*, if the phrase means what it says, to be devoted to pupils' acquisition of more understanding (of whatever kind seems relevant)—by explanation, discussion, and experience. But there are, of course, *other* goods that are not, or not so directly, connected with learning. We wish to keep our children (and ourselves) safe, self-confident, healthy, and so forth: these objectives can, sometimes, be achieved without their *learning* very much.

The difficulty is that these two different kinds of goods may conflict: it may, for instance, very obviously be *dangerous* to learn (or even to try to learn) certain things in the sexual area as in other areas. Settling such conflicts would, presumably, involve trying to weight the goods in the light of some overall criterion such as happiness. I say "presumably" because there seem to be some people who hold so strongly to some nonutilitarian ideal (perhaps in this case an ideal of 'purity', or obeying the 'dark forces in the blood', or whatever) that they are not prepared to cash out this ideal in any other terms: for such people one *just ought* to behave sexually in this or that way, irrespective of whether it makes for one's own or anyone else's happiness. With such people one cannot argue, since there is no agreement on what counts as a good reason; and, indeed, it is difficult—if *all* connection with happiness is severed—to see these "ultimate positions" or "absolute values" as much more than a set of personal preferences, compulsions, or fantasies dressed up in metaphysical clothes.[2] For those of us who are prepared to negotiate on a more reasonable basis, the weighting of different kinds of goods—educational and noneducational—must be taken seriously.

I think much would be gained, in fact, simply by keeping the distinction clearly in mind. At least *some* time and resources could then be devoted to each class of goods, and we should know what we are supposed to be doing in each case (just as, in religious education, it might be acceptable for time and money to be spent in promoting some particular religion or ideal, provided that there was *also* provision for the more strictly educational enterprise of encouraging children to learn and develop more rationality in the area of religion and ideals in general). But, as this parallel shows, there may still be conflicts: the *very idea* of trying to question or learn about certain things will be thought, by some people, to involve some kind of danger to the young.

Since learning and understanding is always *prima facie* desirable, there is of course some onus on those who claim to spot danger: they have to show that the danger is real and not imaginary. This is just the problem that faces those who are worried about "corruption" and "permissiveness": they have to show that some actual damage is done, which is not easy. In the sexual area certain cases would not be seriously in dispute—those, for instance, involving physical harm or trespass on individual liberty (rape is at least that, whatever else it may be). These cases do not cover much ground, however, and our concepts are not really clear enough to negotiate many others. 'Shock' might be mentioned in a case where (for instance) a young child was put into a state of traumatic paralysis by some sexual exhibition; here we should say that palpable damage was being done. On the other hand, certain people may be 'shocked' by exhibitions in a way that, though not ideal, may nevertheless be educationally desirable for them: there is a clear sense in which 'shock', not only in sex education, can be a useful pedagogic tool.

How far can what might be called "threats to one's self-image" or 'alarming invasions of privacy" be counted as genuine damage? For these, unfortunately, cover most of the cases that prevent us from learning as much in the area of sexuality as we ought. We can, again, deal easily with extreme cases: if a timid girl's first sexual experience put her off men for life, we should disapprove; but if such an experience, though involving some "threat" and "invasion," nevertheless, developed her understanding without wrecking her security, we might approve. Few cases are as clear as this.

We are inclined to say here that matters "should be left to the individual" in education as in adult relationships. If a child, or an adult, finds some aspect of sexuality *so* threatening or alarming that he wants to opt out of it, let him so opt. The general John Stuart Mill-type principle behind this is, of course, sound enough, but there are two reasons why it does not solve our problem in the case of education. First, we do in fact *compel* children to learn all sorts of things, even if they very much dislike doing so, on the grounds that we have some kind of mandate over them in their own interests—and why should sex education be peculiarly optional? Second, although we may make no overtly compelling *rules* that enforce attendance or participation in whatever the content of sex education may be, nevertheless, there will be certain semicompulsive pressures exerted on individuals—from their parents, or their peer group, or whomever, if not from the teachers themselves (just as, for teenagers, it may in a particular group be regarded as improper to have sexual experiences or unsporting not to).

Only an effective *tradition* within the school can overcome these difficulties. By this I mean that the educators must be able to provide, not just bits and pieces of a "course in sex education" but a background of community life that encourages such education and makes whatever is necessary for it less threatening to the individual pupil. It is crucially important here that the nature of the tradition—the whole orientation toward sexuality both in theory and practice—should be in the hands of educators and not of other parties, valuable though those other parties would be in a consultative role. Naturally, this would involve a great deal of prior negotiation, if teachers are to have the necessary scope. But if they do not—if schools are not potent enough to form proper communities with proper traditions—then the whole of moral education, not only sex education, is rendered superficial. We have to initiate children and adolescents into a form of *life* (not just a form of thought) in which they will be able to learn a proper relationship to their own bodies and those of other people. The first thing here is that teachers themselves should be clear about what that form of life would look like, which in turn depends on being clear about the relevant concepts. After that, of course, there will be a long political battle to persuade the general public and the politicians who are supposed to represent it. But at least we can make a start.

NOTES

1. See John Wilson, *Practical Methods of Moral Education* (London: Heinemann, 1971), pt. 4; idem, *Education in Religion and the Emotions* (London: Heinemann, 1971), pt. 2 and aps.

2. John Wilson, *A Preface to the Philosophy of Education* (London: Routledge & Kegan Paul, 1979).

ABOUT THE AUTHOR

JOHN WILSON is lecturer and tutor at the Oxford University Department of Educational Studies and Research Supervisor of the Warborough Trust. He has held academic posts at the King's School, Canterbury; Trinity College, Toronto; and the University of Sussex.

He has published some fifteen books and a great number of articles in the field of moral psychology, psychology and education, and is a leading authority in the field of value education.

He was educated at Winchester College and New College, Oxford, where he gained a first-class degree in philosophy.

DATE DUE

GAYLORD

PRINTED IN U.S.A.